Before First Contact

The story of San Diego, before it was San Diego

By Art Fusco

Table of Contents

The Inhumanity of Humanity:
A Trigger Warning

Part One: Ancient History

One - Warring Cultures.........................2
Two - Geology....................................20
Three - First Peoples...........................35

Part Two: Conquering the Americas

Four - Christopher Columbus.............49
Five - First American Adventures.......69
Six - Hernan Cortez............................81
Seven - Juan Rodriguez Cabrillo.......108

List of sources...................................123

The Inhumanity of Humanity:
A Trigger Warning

If you are fragile, this book will break you. This book is not intended to be "safe"; it contains detailed descriptions of some of the atrocities that have shaped our culture. The story is about San Diego before it was San Diego, but the point of this story centers on the Darwinism of cultures and is not intended to be a celebration of these events, just a telling.

Cultures seem to have lives of their own. They're born, they grow, they fight to survive and they die. The birth and death of a culture are not only significant historical subjects to cover, but they are also usually very bloody. It is difficult to separate the two and to do so dramatically impacts the lessons within. If an event doesn't somehow impact us, we don't put much thought into the consequences of said event.

Something that is missing from a lot of modern history are the feelings these events created in those who experienced them. The next few generations may have heard of the events, but those feelings are gone by then. We forget the pain or joy it created and ultimately, fail to consider it when moving through our lives.

This author believes that attempting to protect oneself from the inhumanity of humanity is a noble idea, but carries the unintended consequence of shielding oneself from potential life lessons. It can become a bubble where information and wisdom stagnates. However, aware of the cultural sensibilities of the modern day, the choice has been made to add this little disclaimer:

This book contains graphic descriptions of bigotry and racism. It contains the racism against Africans, which gave birth to a slave trade, and the racism against Native Americans, that dramatically reduced their numbers and destroyed their cultures. It speaks of the hubris and abuse by leaders, explorers and natives. It yells of unspeakably uncomfortable situations that none of us would ever want to experience.

This book speaks about theft. It tries to explain in some detail, the grim consequences of intolerance and the absence of justice. It screams over the removal of limbs, and of innocence, mourns over rape and discrimination, and cries over the descriptions of war and genocide. There are also some hints of this author's gallows humor peppered throughout the book, used as a defense mechanism for dealing with such a heavy subject.

Some might say that the story could be told in a way that does not depict all of the sadness and that could be true, but it would also be misleading. Christopher Columbus did not prove that the Earth was round, nor did he discover America. However, many people still believe these things about him because of the way we taught about him to our youth. It's easy to romanticize events you're far away removed from and so I will attempt to bridge the gap and show some of the ugly details. If you are fragile, this book will break you, but it will also teach you.

-A.F.

Part One:
Ancient History

One - Warring Cultures

"(T)he web of our history is woven of many separate threads, none of these is without' influence in making the color and substance of the whole fabric." - William E. Smythe

First Thread

Two brothers, their father and a small crew were out on a wooden ship in a small sea, mending their fishing nets. If you've been out at sea during a calm day, it can be pretty quiet and peaceful, so I'm not sure why, but when a man came to the brothers and asked them to join him, they bid their father good-bye and left with the man. The brother's names were John and James, the name of the sea was Galilee and the name of the mysterious man they left with was Jesus of Nazareth.

These brothers became apostles of Jesus and witnessed miracles such as the resurrection of Jairus' daughter:

"While he yet spake, there cometh one from the ruler of the synagogue's house, saying to him, Thy daughter is dead; trouble not the Master. But when Jesus heard it, he answered him, saying, Fear not: believe only, and she shall be made whole. And when he came into the house, he suffered no man to go in, save Peter, and James, and John, and the father and the mother of the maiden. And all wept, and bewailed her: but he said, Weep not; she is not dead, but sleepeth. And they laughed him to scorn, knowing that she was dead. And he put them all out, and took her by the hand, and called, saying, Maid, arise. And her spirit came again, and she arose straightway: and he commanded to give her meat. And her parents were

astonished: but he charged them that they should tell no man what was done." - King James Bible, Luke 8:49-56

That wasn't the only "miracle" they witnessed. John, James and another apostle named Peter, were also the only ones to witness the "transfiguration" of Jesus:

"And after six days Jesus taketh Peter, James, and John his brother, and bringeth them up into an high mountain apart, And was transfigured before them: and his face did shine as the sun, and his raiment was white as the light." - King James Bible, Matthew 17:1-2

At one point, a small village of Samaritans decided not to receive Jesus. Upset at the snub and apparently having fiery tempers, the brothers suggested to Jesus that he call down fire and brimstone upon the town.

Jesus didn't like that idea:

"They went, and entered into a village of the Samaritans, to make ready for him. And they did not receive him, because his face was as though he would go to Jerusalem. And when his disciples James and John saw this, they said, Lord, wilt thou that we command fire to come down from heaven, and consume them, even as Elias did? But he turned, and rebuked them, and said, Ye know not what manner of spirit ye are of. For the Son of man is not come to destroy men's lives, but to save them. And they went to another village." - King James Bible, Luke 9:52-56

After Jesus' crucifixion, one of the brothers, James, left and found himself preaching the gospel in a place called Galicia on the

Northwestern tip of the Iberian Peninsula. He decided to travel there because as best as he knew, nobody there had heard of the gospel yet. He did not get many converts while he was there, but then in January of 40 CE, it is said that while he preached, the Virgin Mary appeared to him on top of a pillar. He took it as a sign and returned to the Middle East, but King Herod managed to capture him and in the year 44, killed him:

"Now about that time Herod the king stretched forth his hands to vex certain of the church. And he killed James the brother of John with the sword." - King James Bible, Acts 12:1-2

His remains were returned to Galicia for burial. With the executions of both Jesus and James by Roman officials, Christianity was off to a rough and bloody start, but by February of around 280, the religion had taken over the Roman Empire, replacing Hellenism.

This is the first of many ancient threads that weave into great stories about what happens when cultures clash. Cultures take a long time to develop and they usually do so in isolation, so when they meet with other cultures, their differences stick out and they usually don't understand one another. Sometimes one culture simply wants something the other culture has, such as land, or food. They may not be able to communicate with each other however, thus they may not be able to empathize or trust either. Instead, they'll either dismiss, or try to change each other, leading to theft, culture wars, and sometimes, genocide. The Jewish and Roman reaction to the rise of Jesus was to kill him and later his apostle and followers, yet in the end, one of the most lasting legacies of the Roman Empire would be the Christian faith. Once it dominated the Roman Empire, Christianity began to clash with other cultures. These writings follow the pattern.

The story of the Apostle James is ground in the New Testament, and he is probably the first martyr for Christianity. His name also becomes the root of our subject: If you take the name "James" and translate it into the language at the time, Latin, you will get "Iacomus" (Pronounced EYAH kah mus). The Iberian Peninsula, where James went to preach, had another name: Hispania (his PAN yah).

There were two large cities in Hispania, Cordoba was established in 206 BCE as the Roman capital and Bracara Augusta, now in Subi lands, was established in 20 BCE. Other cities included Toledo and Seville. Hispania was a western frontier in the enormous Roman Empire until about 395 CE, when the last emperor to rule a united Rome died and his sons split the empire in two: The Eastern half, which held Constantinople, was ruled by Arcadius, while the Western half, which held Rome and Hispania, was ruled by a ten year old named Honorius. Hispania became part of the Western Roman Empire, but Roman dominance over the region fell away. By 418, Hispania had broken up into four independent kingdoms, besides the land the Visigoths owned, another group called the Vandals ruled the southernmost part of Hispania.

Meanwhile, in the east, a Gothic man named Alaric became angry when neither emperor offered him a command, so he raised his own army and became the first king of the Visigoths. They then began to invade surrounding lands. While that was going on, a threat of raids by Attila the Hun set the stage for the Bishop of Rome, Leo I, to become the very first Pope by the order of Constantinople. By 493, the Visigoths had traveled to the Italian peninsula from the Germanic region, sacked Rome and continued west taking over a substantial portion of Hispania.

During the middle ages, pilgrimages from Judea to Hispania, in the style of James' biblical trip, became popular and James soon became venerated as Saint James of Spain. Each saint was given a feast date where they would be celebrated, his was July 25th. The Latin language, would become the root language of Italian, Castilian (future Spanish), French, Portuguese and Romanian. English and Germanic languages would come from what the Romans called Germania; Tribal groups who managed to resist Roman rule. A variation of James' Latin name, "Iacomus" developed into "Iago" (EYE AW go), and later "Yago" (YA go). "San Yago" was how one would refer to Saint James at that time.

In 535, a volcano in Indonesia named "Krakatoa" erupted, causing a cloud of ash to wrap around the world that took about eighteen months to settle. Once the dust settled in 542, the Black Death, or Bubonic plague, spread in Constantinople killing thousands and would spread as far as Gaul. In 551, The Eastern Roman Empire decided to team up with the Lombards to take back Ravenna and Rome. The battle was a success and thus most of Italy was taken back by the Eastern Roman Empire. The next year, the Eastern Empire was also able to take the southern coast of Hispania. By 600, the Visigoths lost their capital city of Toulouse to Burgundy who pushed them completely into Hispania. The island of Britannia, like Hispania, had broken into several independent kingdoms when Pope Gregory the Great sent Augustine I to the island to convert the people there into Christianity.

Second Thread

From its Jewish roots, Christianity grew to become larger than Jesus, or what was left of the Roman Empire; it became the dominant culture. Yet down in the Arabian Peninsula, a new culture was springing from similar roots. In 610, a man named Muhammad, living in a village called Mecca, claimed to have seen a vision of the Angel Gabriel while he was asleep. The Angel Gabriel appointed Muhammad Prophet of God (or Prophet of Allah) and tasked him with spreading messages from the Angels to the public. It took him a few years to catch on, but Muhammad was able to pass along these messages and grow his followers, beginning the rise of a new culture.

Of course, when new cultures rise, they begin to clash with the dominant culture. In this case, the ruling classes of Mecca felt as though their culture was threatened. They attacked Muhammad's followers in the streets and generally ostracized them from society. Many followers began to leave Mecca, but Muhammad stayed while his family relocated to a ghetto, where his wife would die in 619. After her death, Muhammad claimed to have received a new prophesy, permitting him and his followers to fight back against the people who were oppressing them. Now threatened, the ruling class then conspired to assassinate Muhammad, forcing him on September of 622 to sneak out of his friend's home and flee to a city called Medina, becoming the "Ummah".

Here in Medina, free from the dominance of the Meccan tribes, the religion of Islam would continue to grow and develop. Muhammad entered the city with so much sway, he became a de-facto ruler, so his prophesies and the way he legislated his city habitually intertwined with each other. Citywide prayers occurred five times a day and giving to the poor became a matter of law. Initially, he established equal rights between men and women, Jews and Arabs promising to protect them, but he was hoping that the entire population of Medina would join the Ummah. He began to receive messages saying that Allah was the same god that the Jews and Christians worshiped and that they would all enter the same paradise, but this didn't convince the Jews to convert. Either frustrated, or threatened by this, Jewish tribes were driven out one by one, one tribe for not wanting to take part in raids. Finally, Muhammad gave the remaining Jews the choice to either convert to Islam or die: They chose to die. They beheaded the men, while the women and children became slaves: Another example of how volatile colliding cultures can be.

Muhammad made it a point to raid passing caravans, mostly from Mecca, to keep his people fed and supplied. In one major raid on a Meccan caravan in March of 624, Muhammad said that anybody who died in the battle would enter paradise, no questions asked. The Meccans were driven back, and Muhammad returned to Medina with a good chunk of supplies from the caravan.

Over a period, Meccan attitudes towards Muhammad and Medina softened. Faced with possible annihilation, the people of Mecca now wanted a truce. By 630, now with an army of ten thousand, Muhammad approached Mecca and took it over without any bloodshed. Muhammad now ruled over Mecca as well as Medina. He died just two years later and controversy followed over who would succeed him and become the next ruler of the Ummah. They chose Muhammad's father-in-law from his second marriage, Abu Bakr, however many Muslims had wanted to appoint his son-in-law, Abu Talib, instead. The future split between Shiites and Sunnis is rooted in this controversy, but at this time, even though Abu Talib disputed the appointment, he eventually threw his support behind Abu Bakr, who became the new Caliph.

Under Abu Bakr, and a later Caliph named Umar, the Muslims subdued surrounding tribes and Islam began to spread across the Arabian Peninsula. By the second half of the century, the followers of Muhammad would grow into an empire that encompassed the whole Peninsula, before heading east to Indian lands, absorbing the Persian Empire along the way and trying to take Constantinople but failing, before turning back and conquering Egypt and then the rest of North Africa. They called the Muslims of North Africa "Berbers".

Conquering Egypt was a big deal, because the city of Alexandria contained the largest repository of information in the ancient world. By this time, Christian rulers had long shut down the philosophy academies in Athens, but the heavy trade routes between Athens and Alexandria ensured the survival of Plato and Aristotle's writings. While most of Christian Europe had entered the dark ages, Muslims in the Middle East had acquired the wisdom of the ancients through conquest.

Among this quest for world domination between these two cultures came a suggestion that the world may be a little larger than once thought. In another part of the world, a seventh century Chinese book named "The Book of Liang" told of a land to the east on the other side of the Pacific Ocean named "Fusang", after a popular plant that was found there and used by the natives of that region. The land was described as arid, but full of native people with traditions that were nothing like the Chinese had ever witnessed, though it is doubtful that this land was in the Americas, for the text speak of a bronze age culture, while the natives of North America were closer to stone.

Thousands of years later, from the other side of the ocean, near the future Colorado River in North America, there was a legend told by the natives of men in ships with golden figureheads. The men claimed they had come from the other side of the ocean.

When around seven thousand Berbers, now part of the Umayyad Caliphate, entered Hispania via the straits of Gibraltar in the year 711, the Visigoths were in the mists of a civil war. The Berbers defeated the divided Visigoths in the battle of Guadalete, giving them a foothold into the Peninsula. Over the next ten years, they would expand to take over all of Hispania, but were defeated by the Franks in the battle of Toulouse on 721, stopping the Islamic advance from entering Europe any further. Hispania had become "Al Andalus", which meant "Land of the Vandals".

However, there was a small band of resisters to the north called the "Asturians". Over the next decades, they'll grow into their own state and eventually be called "Leon". In 756, Abd al-Rahman I defeated the existing Muslim rulers, becoming Prince of the area and turning the Islamic Emirate into the Emirate of Cordoba. Most of Hispania would be under independent Muslim rule for the next seven hundred years.

The Twist

Remember when the Jews felt so threatened by Jesus, they sent the Romans to kill him, or when Muhammad forced the last remaining Jews in Medina to either convert or die? Remember what I said about patterns? With that in mind, you may be asking yourself, "How did living under Islam over hundreds of years affect the inhabitants of what was now called "Al Andalus?" If you're living in the time of this author, you might be surprised, but this pattern is broken here.

Perhaps by then, religious ideas had evolved and become more inclusive, or the transition from living in deserts to living on rich fertile land altered their perspectives. Perhaps it was the size, strength, and stability of the Muslim lands as a whole that gave them the confidence to accept other cultures, or maybe, with their knowledge of ancient wisdom, they took a page from Alexander the Great and allowed other cultures to thrive as long as they acknowledged their inferiority to those who ruled over them. Though many Iberian inhabitants converted to Islam after the Muslims came and took over, there seemed to be legitimate acceptance of other cultures during this time. The Muslims that lived and ruled in Spain were called "Moors" and under them, academics thrived. Arabic became the new language of the intellectuals. The Moors were curious about the history of this lush and fertile land and of the land around it.

Now that Muslims had legitimized themselves on the world stage, it seems as though they took a break from conquering lands in order to grow intellectually. They set up colleges called "madrasas" around the peninsula. They began to mass-produce paper and used that paper to write books and encourage literacy. There were new inventions such as the astrolabe, which was a way to measure the inclination of stars and planets in order to tell local time, like an ancient watch; as well as a material called "endrime", which is similar to denim.

Architecture, irrigation, astronomy, history, mathematics, poetry, even something that would later split into science and philosophy were all improved as scholars translated the ancient texts recovered from Alexandria into Arabic. Cordoba grew into one of the largest cities in Europe with mosques, bell towers and about seventy libraries, peppering their skyline. Elsewhere in the peninsula, other new cities would emerge, including Madrid and Granada.

Arched columns shaded the streets during the day, with flame-lanterns installed on them that would light up during the night. Homes became equipped with running water and thus, courtyards were soon filled with lush gardens. The echoes of the greatest minds of Ancient Greece, Egypt, and the Roman Empire as a whole were like thin strands of thread that were being spun together to create a new and more robust culture. Under hundreds of years of Muslim rule, the people of Al Andalus experienced an enlightenment.

Also during this time, the holdings of Asturias in the north were growing. By the time it became Leon in 911, it had taken over about a third of the peninsula. The land of the Franks had split into two and was continuing to form their own identities, the Vikings had invaded Europe through Normandy and the vast empire the Muslims had gained split into factions.

By the year 1095, Constantinople was in threat of being taken over and they asked the Pope for help. In response, the Pope called for the first Crusade: A general call to arms for Christians to join against the Muslims. For the next four years, scores of Christians from France, The Holy Roman Empire, and Naples met at Byzantium and pushed back the Sultanate of Rum. The Christians of Hispania didn't participate however, it seems like they were having problems of their own. The tiny Christian resistance at the top of the Iberian Peninsula had grown so large; it now covered about half of the peninsula, taking over cities like Toledo. Toledo gave up without a fight, so the city was spared from destruction and for at least a little while, Muslims and Christians lived side by side. Finally, in 1140, a new faction broke off from Leon the new country was Portugal.

An excerpt of the preface of Susan Wise Bauer's History of the

Renaissance World tells a story of a man who visited Toledo a little after 1140. He came looking for an ancient astronomy book and soon stayed to translate anything that interested him:

"Not long after 1140, A.D., the Italian scholar, Gerard of Cremona traveled to the Spanish Peninsula, hoping to find a rare copy of the thousand year old Greek astronomy text known as the Almagest. His chances were better there than anywhere else in Europe. The southern half of the peninsula had been in Arab hands for centuries, and the ruling dynasties of Muslim Spain had brought with them thousands of classical texts. Translated into Arabic, but long lost to the vernacular languages of the west. The libraries of the city of Toledo, in the center of the peninsula, housed scores of these valuable volumes, and Toledo had now been recaptured by one of the Christian kingdoms of the north, meaning that western scholars could visit it in relative safety.

Gerard found more than he bargained for: Not just astronomy texts, but classical and Arabic studies of dialectic, geometry, philosophy and medicine. Unknown monographs by Euclid, Galen, Ptolemy and Aristotle, a whole treasury of knowledge. Overwhelmed, he settled into Toledo and set to work learning Arabic. 'Regretting the poverty of the Latins in these things', one of his students wrote, 'he learned the Arabic language in order to be able to translate. To the end of his life, he continued to transmit to the Latin world, as if to his own beloved heir. Whatever books he thought finest in many subjects as actively and as plainly as he could.' Renaissance had begun." - Susan Wise Bauer

This author went into certain depths here not only to explain culture clashes between Muslims and Christians, or to highlight early cultural influences that would influence the creation of future San Diego, but to point out that it is here, where the ancient wisdom that the Muslims took from Alexandria and preserved for centuries, would be "rediscovered" by Christian Europe. This treasure trove of information formed the basis of our earliest known stories, and a vast pool of early scientific knowledge. It gave future generations a sense of adventure and it has even lead future explorers to travel the most remote regions of the world in search of long lost cities where some of these events took place. The culture that would help influence the creation of future San Diego was also the culture that provided that massive service to the rest of the world and to future generations, that culture was Islam.

Many modern English words have their root in the Arabic language because of this time, from "alcohol" to "chemistry", from "assassin" to "lime". "Algebra", another subject that was translated into Latin from Arabic during this time, explained of a mathematical concept called "sifr", or empty, the precursor to the modern zero. Our modern numbers also come from Arabic.

The author really wishes to press on about how big of a deal this was to our overall culture: Europeans returned to their countries full of ancient, translated works and started founding colleges and universities such as Oxford. These old works were carefully taught and studied at these new colleges, universities, even hospitals. The knowledge brought back from Toledo made the rest of the world self-aware of its collective past, and made the western world wiser.

Soon scholars in these new universities would study these documents and write about them, building upon that knowledge and from it, asking new questions. They began to produce new works and even analyze the works of the ancients. In time, Christians living on the Iberian Peninsula such as the Portuguese, learn about the rest of the world and want to create their own adventures.

We have become the heirs of an ancient intellectual movement that began in the ancient cities of Sumer and continued throughout Egyptian, Greek, and Roman times.

A second Crusade was launched in 1146 and lasted until 1149, with the warring Iberians once again staying out. In 1158, a new faction broke away from Leon, named Castile. A third Crusade took place from 1189 to 1192, and a fourth from 1202 to 1204. The battle of Las Navas de Tolosa occurred in 1212, giving Castile a portion of Muslim land. Between the fourth and fifth Crusades, the Kingdom of Castile continued to grow, and by 1231, devoured Leon, becoming a powerful kingdom. There was another battle in 1236 which took Cordoba for Castile, another one in 1245 that took Jaen and another one in 1248 that took Seville until all that was left was the city of Granada - The Moors had become the minority.

In 1300, Pope Boniface the Eighth had formalized a yearlong celebration started in Roman times called the Jubilee, where every fifty years, prisoners were freed and debts were forgiven. To the north, Amsterdam was first declared an official city. A "Book of the Marvels of the World" was published that year. Dictated to his cellmate while imprisoned, the book describes the extravagant travels of a man named Marco Polo through the Middle East and the orient, including his time with Kublai Khan of the Mongol Empire. The book also speaks of a large ancient city that lay to the islands east of the Empire named "Cipango".

Cipango is Japan. Polo's book became a bestseller and widely influential. Thirsting for adventure and wealth, travels to the Far East became more frequent for trading exotic objects such as silk. With the increase of demand, routes through the Middle East, later known as the Silk Road, became more expensive to cross. Because of this, people began looking for other ways to reach the orient.

The Weave

Though the seeds of our future city were planted back in biblical times, it isn't until around 1400 when we first begin to see the seed sprout. By then, kingdoms in Romania were resisting Ottoman invasions, and all of Europe had an estimated population of about fifty two million people. In Seville, a city said to be founded in ancient times by Hercules after sailing through the Strait of Gibraltar, there laid a small village named San Nicolás del Puerto. Within that village was a pious couple who had just added to the population by giving birth to a healthy baby boy. By then, the name "San Yago" had morphed into "Santiago", the boy's parents decided to use a shorter, more masculine version of it: "Diego". This child will be the man that our future city will be named after - though nobody knows that yet.

There really isn't much known about Diego, and he wasn't a large figure in life. He was a rather quiet boy who ended up embracing the hermit life and finding religion in his adulthood. He soon became a lay brother at the Order of Friars Minor. In 1445, he was sent to the Canary Islands, a group of islands just west of the African coast, which had just been rediscovered, to help convert the natives in the area to Christianity. Diego later returned to Castile in 1450 to share in Pope Nicholas the Fifth's Jubilee Year celebrations and attended the canonization of Bernardine of Siena. Diego then spent about three months at the Basilica of Santa Maria, caring for the sick, where it is told that many miraculous cures took place and were recorded. He spent the remainder of his life in solitude at the Friary of Santa Maria de Jesus in Alcala. An abscess took Diego's life on November 12, 1463. However, the smell that emitted from his infection and from his corpse was of a pleasant fragrance and he didn't begin to rot or undergo rigor-mortis for days afterwards, according to accounts.

This wouldn't be the last time Diego's remains made headlines. Shortly after his death, while on a hunting trip... anywhere between 1463 and 1474, King Henry the Fourth of Castile had fallen off his horse and hurt his arm. The pain was so intense, that he didn't know what to do and nobody knew how to treat his pain, so apparently in his agony, and remembering the stories of "miraculous cures" and whatever, he decided to head to Alcala and pray to Diego. They even removed Diego's remains from the casket so that the King could kiss his body and place his skeletal remains of a hand on his injured arm. It apparently worked, according to the King.

Henry's pain went away and Diego was placed back into rest. A chapel was later built in 1485 and 1514 in his hometown. His remains are kept at a Cathedral in Alcala de Hernares in Madrid, and it is put on display every year during the time of his feast: November 13th.

While Diego was living his life, the kingdoms throughout the peninsula began expeditions looking for wealth and trade. Mostly, they were looking for inexpensive ways to reach the lands to the east. In 1402, African people were discovered living in the Canary Islands and a French explorer decided that they needed Jesus. He set up an expedition and captured some of the inhabitants, brought them back and sold them as slaves. He then went to Castile and asked to become King of the Canaries under Castile, with the intention of converting the inhabitants to Christianity. This request was granted but instead of converting these natives, most of them were sold off as slaves and replaced by Castilians like Diego. Presto! Islands converted.

Portugal wanted their own little empire, so they decided to attack a North African city named Ceuta and were instantly successful, but spent the next few years defending it, which got expensive. They began looking for other ways to reach the east and so started sailing further and further south, down the western coast of the African Continent.

This had been the furthest south any Christian had ever sailed. At first they didn't find anybody, but once he reached the Azores, they found villages of Moors. They took them and brought them back to Portugal where they sold them off to slavery. They made so much money off of doing that, other explorers began sailing past the Azores.

After finding a decent port, sailors would anchor, map the area, then ride horses inland until they found a village of people and kidnapped them - men, woman and children. The African parents would of course freak out and resist, so the Portuguese would take their children onto the ships, giving the parents little choice but to follow them on. Sometimes, rivers were so large, they could take long boats and row inland, happily displacing more families as they advanced. Anyone who resisted seizure was killed.

By 1444, six large ships sailed from the Portuguese city of Lagos with the intent of stealing more people, as well as their property, and selling them off. They returned with two hundred and fifty Africans and sold them right on the dock, breaking up many families right then and there: Mothers and fathers who tried to protect their children by following them onto the ships were now trapped on a new continent and would now never see their children again and for the rest of their own lives be forced to live under servitude. How would you manage under those conditions?

But at least they now have a chance to go to Heaven when they die. Sounds shitty, but that seems to be the mentality back then: If you have to suffer some to get to heaven, then suffer you will. They thought these native Africans were dirty and living in damnation and that at least as slaves, they would be dressed and civil. In 1452, the King of Portugal asked the Pope to sanction his actions as a crusade, "a holy war on the enemies of the Church". The Pope agreed and released a papal bull called "Dum Diversas" making the perpetual enslavement of non-Christians into law.

By 1492, Castile would be successful in ousting the last of the Jews and Muslims from the peninsula, but that would never be enough to satisfy the god of the Christians...

Two – Geology

Tectonic Plates

"Differentiation" is a term that has a little bit to do with geology, and a little bit with cosmology. In space, a giant ball of molten rock has a lot of convection going on inside, where heavier elements sink to the middle of the ball and stay molten due to the pressure, while lighter elements rise to the surface and cool at a faster rate. Differentiation is what created the Earth's core, mantle, and crust. As the Earth's cooled crust sat on top of a thick layer of flowing rock, the surface started to crack, dividing the crust into several tectonic plates that glide across the surface of the mantle from the convection it creates. These plates will eventually arrange themselves into several supercontinents that will break up and reform to make the continents we see today.

Hundreds of millions of years ago, all of the tectonic plates were joined into one large landmass, called Pangaea. One of these plates, the North American Plate, was in the Midwestern corner of the super-continent, and the Pacific Plate was just a micro plate south of the enormous Farallon Plate. In time, convection caused volcanic activity that influenced the growth of the Pacific Plate. This growth pushed the Farallon Plate aside towards the west, which in turn, pushed up arcs of volcanic islands through the water at its edges. These islands drifted westward, before crashing into the northwestern corner of the North American Plate, breaking off from the Farallon, and forming the lands of Guatemala, Chipas, Oaxaca, Veracruz, Tlaxcala, Morelos, Guerrero, Mexico City, Hidalgo, Michoacan, Queretaro, Guanajuato, Colima, Jalisco, Nayarit, Aguascalientes, San Luis Potosi, Zacatecas, Tamaulipas, Sinaloa, Durango, Nuevo Leon, Coahuila, Chihuahua, Sonora, Baja California, and Baja California

Sur. The formation continues up to Arizona, New Mexico, Colorado, Wyoming, and Montana, up through Canada's Alberta, Northwest and Yukon territories as well as Alaska. Then south to the lands of British Colombia, Washington, Oregon and Upper California, which looked very different as the land was flatter than it is today.

About two hundred million years ago, a fault line appeared between the areas of land that are now called New Jersey and Morocco. This marked the breakup of Pangaea and over time, the rift between the two lands separated more and more, eventually filling with water and giving birth to oceans: First the Tethys, then the Atlantic.

While Pangaea was beginning to break up, an extinction event occurred which allowed the first evolving dinosaurs to begin their reign on the planet. Though we don't know how the event occurred, the most reasonable explanation was some form of climate change. Ocean levels rose, the climate became hot and muggy from pole to pole, and the first pebbles and rocks to make up San Diego did not exist yet. Ninety million years ago, the Midwest portion of the North American Plate was covered by an ancient sea, separating the arcs of land to the far west from the lands to the east: North America actually looked like two mountainous continents, the Rockys and the Alleghenys separated by an ocean.

Over time, rain and snowfall in the mountain regions allowed ancient rivers and beach tides to erode away the high peaks very slowly, and mud and sediment from this erosion washed downstream into the ancient Paleo-Pacific Ocean, making deep ocean beds shallower and shallower. As sea levels later fell, it slowly exposed the Midwest and joined the east to the west once again.

The North American plate was drifting west, while the Farallon Plate, pushed by the growing Pacific micro plate, was moving east. Eventually, the Farallon Plate began to sink under the southwestern edge of the North American Plate, creating an off shore trench. The push also caused underwater land between the trench and the coast to rise up from the sea into a new arc of ancient volcanoes. The active volcanoes spread ash and sediment onto the Farallon Plate as it continued to dive underneath the North American Plate, deepening the trench, and heating the rocks under the land into granitic magmas, which were pushed up to the surface through the volcanoes. The metamorphic rock that oozed from these coastal volcanos during the Jurassic Period will make up the future mountains of the Sierra Nevadas, and the Peninsular Region. The Peninsular holds the Cuyamacca and Julian Mountains and started about one hundred and thirty miles south-east of where San Diego presently lies, possibly close to where the Mexican city of San Luis Rio Colorado is today.

During the mountain growth, veins of molten gold were secretly injected into the Julian Mountains and cooled. Mountain growth stopped about ninety million years ago, once the Farallon Plate was completely buried under the North American Plate, but volcanic activity didn't stop until about twenty eight million years ago, when subduction finally ended. These volcanoes probably became extinct at that time.

Rains and freeze/thaw cycles begin to take a toll on the rugged mountains of the Peninsular and the Sierra Nevadas, which began to be eroded by the rains. About seventy five million years ago, the sediment that eroded away from the Cuyamacca Mountains was carried toward the Pacific in streams created by melting snow and rainwaters. The stream cut a gorge through a volcanic remnant called Cowles Mountain. Sediment carried created a small delta, and birthed a proto version of the San Diego River. Likewise, rains eroded from Mount Helix and San Miguel created another delta that would form into Bonita, Chula Vista and National City. A third delta that would grow into Otay and Imperial Beach was created from the sediment eroded from Otay Mountain. As sea levels rose and fell on the beaches, the sediments would layer up. Because the receding water was gradual, river deltas were smoothed into mesas. Though the mountains were now exposed, the inland and coast was still underwater and without form.

K/Pg Boundary

Sixty five million years ago, in an area about three thousand kilometers east from San Diego, a ten kilometer wide meteor or comet barreled into the present-day Yucatan Peninsula, causing global destruction. Earthquakes, volcanic eruptions, and mega tsunamis ensued. The debris from the blast reached Earth's atmosphere and as it rained back down, it became superheated before impacting the surface as fireballs. This also raised the temperature of the atmosphere, ignited mass wildfires, dropped sea levels, which exposed more land, and ultimately triggered the Cretaceous-Paleogene extinction event. The land that was forming into San Diego, being as close as it was to ground zero, may have suffered some fire and brimstone. It may have also experienced a drop in sea levels. When the dust finally settled, three out of four living things on the planet had died, including most of the dinosaurs. This left a thick layer of ash all over the world, which was later buried by sediment, and compacted into what geologists call the K-Pg Boundary.

...and to think this would be the least violent chapter in the book!

By about fifty million years ago, a small system of rivers was beginning to form at this time, which continued to deposit and distribute sediment into new land. One of the rivers up north was the Santa Ysebel, which carved out San Pasqual Valley in the process of draining into the San Dieguito River, which carved through the land before emptying into the Pacific Ocean. As the ocean levels continued to change, the sediment at the mouth of the San Dieguito River was pushed southward by winds and water currents, giving an initial shape to the curving coast and creating its first modern peninsula: Crown Point. Looking south of Crown Point, the sediments that flowed from the Cuyamacca Mountains, was now piling into lowlands that will someday form Point Loma. Still influenced by the rise and fall of ocean levels, winds and currents, erosion on the coastal edges caused pieces of the raised land to fall off of the edges and sink into the ocean, further shaping the coast and creating the cliff edges of Del Mar, La Jolla, and Point Loma, these changes are still evident today.

The mountains of San Diego were finished and exposed, but much of the coastal mesas were still forming underwater. By thirty million years ago, the Pacific and North American Plates finally met and started to grind, giving birth to the eight hundred mile long San Andreas Fault. This also bent the land upward to the west of the San Andreas Fault, but sunk the land where the fault was at, creating the future Salton Sink. In San Diego, many other smaller faults were created in the process, like the Rose Canyon Fault, and the La Nacion Fault system. About six million years ago, because the Pacific Plate continued to grind north, the entire coast of California shifted up the same way, slowly tearing a rift valley between Baja-California and the Mexican mainland, which filled up with ocean water to become the Gulf of California. The ancient Gulf of California covered the

Salton Sink and reached all the way up north to future Indio, California until ocean levels fell again.

Meanwhile, the Rose Canyon Fault started to shift the northern coast of San Diego to the northwest. The shifting faults warped the coastal topography of San Diego, raising Mount Soledad and Point Loma from the waters. The land to the east and south of Point Loma stayed underwater, making it an island and creating an enormous bay from La Jolla, down to the highlands of Imperial Beach and reached as far east as Bonita. The La Nacion Fault is actually a system of slip faults that lower in elevation as you move westward where present day Chula Vista and National City sit. Those lands were still under water and forming.

Three million years ago, the Colorado River, which emptied into the Gulf of California, deposited enough layers of sediment to separate the Salton Sink from the Gulf of California creating a large ancient lake called Lake Cahuilla. To the west, the coastal and inland region of San Diego was still underwater. Movements from the Rose Canyon Fault stretched out the bulge of land in the La Jolla area just above Crown Point. Just to the west of Point Loma, below the waters, a system of cross faults called the Silver Strand, Coronado, and Spanish Bight Faults pushed up two low clumps of land: North Island, and Coronado. Four smaller islands to the southwest were also pushed up by other cross faults in the process: Mexico's Los Coronados Islands. These lands wouldn't be exposed until sea levels once again fell however.

Lake Cahuilla began a cycle of evaporating and refilling, as it dried, it would leave huge layers of salt deposits on the desert sand. By two million years ago, ocean levels dropped dramatically, exposing the smooth land underneath. As water levels dropped a system of creeks and rivers began to cut valleys and canyons into the mesa including the San Diego River, which now extended to Presidio Hill. Rivers that were birthed around this time were Chollas Creek, the San Luis River, the Sweetwater River, the Otay River, and the Tijuana River. Other rivers and creeks carved out Maple Canyon, Cabrillo Canyon, Florida Canyon, Switzer Canyon, Manzanita Canyon, Juniper Canyon, Telegraph Canyon, Paradise Valley and Spring Valley. Thick shrubs and small trees spread out from the mountains to the newly exposed land and valleys. Wild grasses began to cover the eastern half of National City and Chula Vista, now partially exposed.

Five hundred thousand years ago, the flat mesa that would become downtown San Diego was still underwater. An ancient California Grey Whale had died there, possibly beached on shallow waters. As oceans levels continued to recede, its remains were buried, not to be uncovered for half a million years.

First Humans

The extinction of the dinosaurs in the beginning of the Paleogene cleared a path for other life forms to slowly evolve into their places. They started out in Africa as small nocturnal shrew-like creatures, which grew into hominids, then great apes, then early humans, and finally, Homo sapiens. Homo sapiens evolved and spread out across Afro-Eurasia. These humans reached South Asia by about fifty thousand years ago, and reached East Asia by thirty thousand to seventeen thousand years ago. They didn't know that they were migrating across a world. In their perspective, they were simply following the herds of caribou, bison and mammoth that went through their regular migration patterns. They lived where the food lived.

At this point, the Earth's tectonic plates were pretty much where they are today, but the ocean levels still changed the appearance of the land. By about seventeen thousand years ago or about 15,000 BCE, in the area of the world between Alaska and the Siberia called Beringia, the last ice age lowered ocean levels, which allowed these herds, traveling east, to cross the plains of Beringia from Asia onto a whole new continent: North America. By the time this land bridge was swallowed up in the end of the Ice Age, separating the old world from the new, a succession of three waves of humans migrated across the strait. One wave followed the coastline down what would someday be the Provinces of Yukon and British Columbia and the States of Washington and Oregon, adapting to the unique lands and climate of each and making them their new homes. Some migrated further south to the Californias and settled there. Overall, it is estimated that out of the fifty four million natives living in the Americas, ten thousand humans lived in the southern portion of California by the time the Spanish arrived.

By about twelve thousand years ago, some of these people, bringing with them an ancient and little known culture and language, eventually were the first humans in history to discover San Diego. With a large coastal harbor full of shrubs, willow trees cactus and cottonwoods, complete with river valleys, distant mountains and cliffs that protected the area from heavy winds and storms.

Some humans moved on to Central and South America to become the native empires of those regions. Those empires started out as new agrarian societies that took a wild grass with hard little kernels called "teosinte" and over thousands of years, cultivated it into corn. They also learned to plant, beans, squash and eventually potatoes. The Mixtec were established in southern Mexico first. The Olmec soon followed and the Chavin emerged in modern day Puru. The Maya would come to live in the Yucatan Peninsula, created when an asteroid impacted the area, sixty five million years before. The Paracas were located south of the Chavin, and north of the Olmec, the Zapotec was established. Eventually, they learned how to travel to the Caribbean and soon afterwards, the Ciboney appeared in Cuba. Eventually the Olmec, Chavin, and Zapotec cultures disappeared. Paracas becomes Nazca, and from the former Zapotec, comes the ancient city of Teotihuacan.

The Maya began to spread in Central America, and new establishments were made in South America, but by 900 CE, the Maya disappeared and so did the Hiari who had taken over Nazca. The Toltec would take over Teotihuacan and after that, the Aztecs. In South America, the Inca began taking over vast regions of land. By the time the Spanish arrived, the Aztecs were in the mist of wars with various other cultures surrounding their empire.

However, a group of humans did decide to stay in future San Diego and enjoy its climate and abundance of food. These Paleo-Indians named their new home various names according to descriptions of the land such as, "Moc-Nees", which in their language was translated to "Black Land". This is what they called Point Loma, where they would gather clams, mollusks and other forms of abalone. "Cosoy" meant "Drying Out Place" and by then, the once mighty San Diego River had slowed to a trickle. Shrinking dramatically, it left in its place, a five hundred foot inland valley with a relatively muddy flat and hundred-foot floodplain, covered in a variety of greenery and wild life. The land that they inhabited was indeed drying out.

I suppose the best way to describe the San Diego natives of this time would be as "stone aged". They still made their tools out of sticks, stones, shells and bones, and knew little of metals or mining. The slightest flair of a metallic object would fascinate them and they would take rocks with metals that shined, grind them up and use it as face paint. A future archaeologist named Malcolm Jennings Rogers described them as a "scraper maker culture", meaning a majority of tools they used were simple scrapers. However, for over ten thousand years, this worked well for the natives.

These people lived off the land as hunters and gatherers. They would mostly eat shellfish, small game, acorns, and seeds. Some of them were vegetarian. Because of the abundance of food in the area, they had no need to learn about agriculture like those in the south did. The animals they hunted were bison, rabbits, foxes, snakes, mice, crows, coyotes, frogs, and even cray-fish. To hunt, they made traps and used bows and arrows, clubs, spears, and of course, their bare hands. They refused to hunt or eat some animals for religious reasons, such as dogs, bears, and pigeons. At one point, they may have had horses roaming the area, as horses evolved in the Americas but they were probably hunted to near extinction for food, never realizing the true potential of the horse until generations later.

By around ten thousand years ago, a small group of horses managed to escape North America into Asia, over the same land bridge that brought humans into the Americas. In Asia, other humans will learn how to ride and breed them. The horse would go on to help army after army conquer empires throughout human history.

The last of the Columbian Mammoths were still roaming the deserts and coasts during this time, but soon became extinct. One died in future Carlsbad, where the Glen Ridge Apartments are now. Another one died roaming around in future downtown San Diego, directly under the remains of the California Grey Whale that had died two hundred thousand years before, but was now buried under ten feet of sediment. The remains of the mammoth, as well as a treasure trove of abalone, would slowly be buried in twenty more feet of sediment on the grounds where the Thomas Jefferson School of Law now sits. Winds blowing southeast gathered sediment from La Jolla and Pacific Beach and began to spread it southward, and just like in Crown Point, created a small strip of sand that stretched almost all the way to Point Loma. This strip of land would someday become Mission Beach. The San Diego River used to be higher and wider, and would empty its sediments out into the bay, which was only partially separated by Point Loma. Over time, the land between Point Loma and the mouth of the river became shallower and shallower due to the sediment deposits. The deposit from the San Diego River created a flat plain that once again connected Point Loma to the mainland, splitting the huge bay in two, including a crude version of Mission Bay, which at this time is simply swampy ground. San Diego Bay was so shallow, you couldn't sail a large ship past Ballast Point, the finger of land sticking out from Point Loma, without getting beached.

Winds blowing northeast gathered silt and mud that traveled west from the Tijuana River, forming an underwater ridge south of Coronado Island. This ridge connected North Island to Coronado through a small strip of land called the Spanish Bight. The ridge follows the western coast of Coronado Island, and connecting it to the mainland through Imperial Beach. As the ocean levels continued to change, these ridges were exposed, giving birth to the Silver Strand, and turning the islands into a peninsula.

Microclimate and Plant life

San Diego's topography of mountains, canyons, and two bays gave San Diego a microclimate. Normally, cool air comes in from the Pacific and heats up as it moves further inland and over the mountains. As it does, moisture in the air condenses more in the coast than it does inland. This sometimes gives San Diego a thin layer of clouds that will usually cover the coastline area, but dissipates as it moves further inland. Because the temperature is usually cool off the Pacific coast, tropical storms and hurricanes are a rarity. About ten days out of the year or so, winds will come from the opposite direction, the hot eastern deserts, which brings gusts of hot air to the coast, but usually the climate of San Diego is cool and dry with low humidity, raining less than fifty days out of the year.

By now, the mainland was still much wetter than it is today and was thickly covered with shrubs such as yucca, deer-weed, black-mustard, agave, buckwheat, and sages. However, San Diego at this time is mainly a brown and marshy coastal desert. Trees such as oaks, firs, sycamores, cypress, pinyon pines, cottonwoods, and willow trees dotted the area as well. In fact, there was a forest of pinyon pines in the mountain region. There were no palm trees anywhere except the inland desert area. Out of the one hundred and fifty seven species of palm trees that grow in California today, only one species of palm is indigenous to North America: The California Washingtonia, and the closest that it grew is where Anza-Borrego Desert State Park is today. Much of this greenery stretched from the beaches, up the many valleys and into the mountains. The land from Rose Canyon to Point Loma may have once been covered in a thick forest, though evidence suggests that it was covered in the same plants as the rest of the region, though maybe thickly. The rest of the landscape looked barren, with various dry shrubs scattered about. Wild life included rabbits, squirrels, deer, bears, bison, owls, raccoons, skunks, snakes and lizards. Horses and mammoths were long gone.

By about nine thousand years ago – 7000 BCE – San Diego looked pretty close to what it looked like when Spanish settlers first explored it.

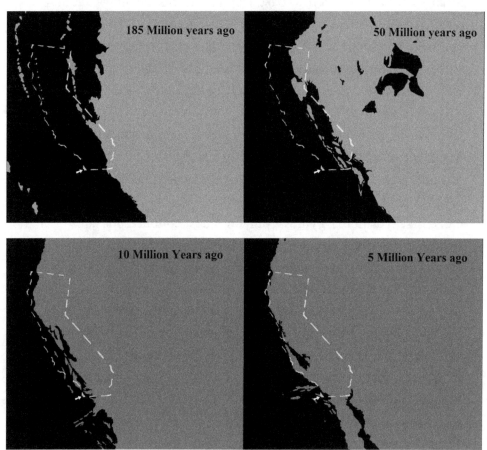

Fig.1-4: Southwest United States,
185 MYA to 5 MYA

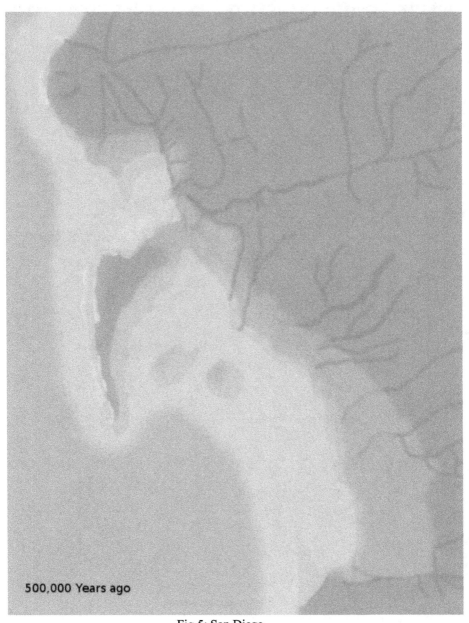

500,000 Years ago

Fig 5: San Diego,
500 TYA

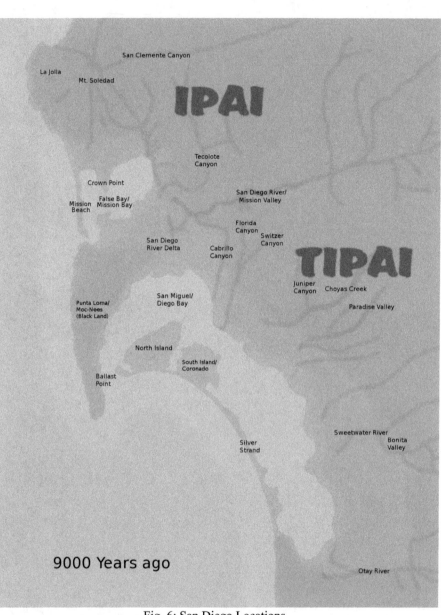

Fig. 6: San Diego Locations,
9 TYA

Three - First Peoples

Story Tellers

"In the beginning there was no earth or land. There was nothing except salt water. This covered everything like a big sea. Two brothers lived under this water. The oldest one was Teaipakomat.

When the elder brother saw that there was nothing, he made first of all little red ants. They filled the water up thick with their bodies and so made land. Then Teaipakomat caused certain black birds with flat bills to come into being. There was no sun or light when he made these birds. So they were lost and could not find their roost. So Teaipakomat took three kinds of clay, red, yellow, and black, and made a round, flat object. This he took in his hand and threw up against the sky. It stuck there. It began to give a dim light. We call it the moon now.

The light was so poor that they could not see very far. So Teaipakomat was not satisfied, for he had it in mind to make people. He took some more clay and made another round, flat object and tossed that up against the other side of the sky. It also stuck there. It made everything light. It is the Sun. Then he took a light-colored piece of clay, and split it up part way. He made a man of it. That is the way he made man. Then he took a rib from the man and made a woman, the first Woman. The children of this man and this woman were people, Ipai.

They lived in the east at a great mountain called Wikami. If you go there now you will hear all kinds of singing in all languages. If you put your ear to the ground you will hear the sound of dancing. This is caused by the spirits of all the dead people, who go back there when

they die and dance just as they do here. That is the place where
everything was created first."
-Kumeyaay creation story

The native people of San Diego County, like other humans who
roamed about the Earth, were story tellers. Language allowed early
humans to pass on information, such as old tales, down from
generation to generation. These tales transformed to myths, and the
myths morphed to legend. They believed their actions determined
their fate, and would tell great stories over a number of days with
lessons in them, sometimes about an afterlife. Some of their stories
have little seeds of Christian mythology like the creation story told
above, for instance. In this one, the man sacrifices a rib to make a
woman out of nowhere. It also tells of the creation of the sun and
moon, but nothing about the land other than it was made up from the
bodies of lots of little red ants. One of these stories are actually
similar to the biblical flood story. It's likely the biblical references
were added later on by the Spanish in an attempt to convert the
natives or the natives could have combined stories. Remembering
these legends became important to the future culture of the people
who inhabited San Diego, for the lessons derived from these legends
would become the basis of their culture and of how they behaved.
These people in particular put their stories to the tune of music -
rather than telling stories, they sang them to each other.

There is, unfortunately, very little information on the stories they
used to pass down. A lot of their past and culture have disappeared
with time, with real interest in preserving it only occurring within the
last fifty years. Only recently have the natives, themselves, been able
to preserve and archive the important aspects of their past. For the
last two hundred years, much of what was known of them was

passed down through the lens of those who intended to change, or to eradicate them.

That may sound harsh, but it's true that for many generations, the San Diego natives were seen as less than human. For instance, if you read William E. Smythe's otherwise wonderful 1914 History of San Diego, the third chapter of the first part is titled "The taming of the Indian". Shaving just a bit off the top, this is how Mr. Smythe described the native San Diegans back then:

"The Indians who swarmed about the bay of San Diego were, apparently, as poor material as ever came to the social mill. All the early observers, except the missionaries, spoke of them with contempt."

Wow! Notice how he used the word "swarmed" as if they were annoying little flies. Remember, the natives had inhabited the land for many thousands of years before surviving through three different governments that were imposed on them by the time Smythe wrote this. They had even survived an attempted genocide by the United States government by then. He continues:

"No one ever called the San Diego Indian 'the noble red man', for he was neither noble nor red, but a covetous, thievish, and sneaking creature, of a brownish complexion, something like the soil. There were no orators among them and, it is to be feared, very few brave men, for when they fought they acted like a pack of cowards."

Double wow! It obviously wasn't seen as racist to speak this way of the natives back in the early 1900s, but today it is probably safe to flat out say that that was pretty racist. This isn't relevant to our history, but can you believe that there is an elementary school in San Ysidro named after this man? Why would anyone allow that? Because history is usually written by the victors and sometimes, it results in biased or ignorant assessments of the defeated. Mr. Smythe therefore left out a lot of potentially useful historical information about them that would have been invaluable to those who would later study them, like this author. His racism has deprived this author and our readers of relevant information regarding the natives and even though the rest of his history is fine, it is easy to resent the lack of relevant information in that third chapter.

No lack of information on this third chapter, however!

The Way They Lived

Once these early humans settled onto the land, about twelve thousand years ago, they began to diversify throughout the area. Figuring out the seasonal patterns, they would migrate out on the coast, during the hotter times of the year and would move back inland, over the peninsular mountains, during the cooler times, so they didn't really have a central living location. They set up temporary villages of grass huts and fire pits across the open territory. They learned to build canoes out of certain plants and would voyage out into the waters, toward one of a number of visible islands, or around the bay, fishing or searching for oysters and mollusks, which used to be abundant in this region.

The agave and yucca plants were some of the more important plants that native people used to live on. When the season was right, they could dry, using a rock, they could harvest the plant and shave yucca or agave plants down to strips of fiber. They would then tie them into ropes, fishing nets and string to make bowls. During the springtime, agave plants could harvested using oak sticks with wedged tips hardened in fire and heated in pits for about a day to be barbecued, making a treat that tasted sweet. Sticks made of oak would be used to dig out whole agave plants. A pit would be dug into the ground and lined with river stones, which would then be heated. Once heated, about fifteen to twenty agave plants, their leave cut off, were placed in the pit with the leaves and buried for a day where they would cook. Each agave pit represented a family.

Using spears and bows with stone arrow heads, they would hunt and gather their food. Over time, they found smarter and more sophisticated ways of hunting. One method of hunting was to burn a small area of brush and wait to catch and kill the animals that ran out of the burning brush and of course, this would fill the skies with smoke and in warmer seasons, would prevent larger brush fires. They usually caught small animals, but were not afraid to hunt larger ones. They used fire for ceremonies, for heat and to cook meat from what they killed. They would use the skin of killed animals as blankets, or as clothing, though the males usually went around naked if it wasn't too cold, while the women usually wore something. Besides agave and yucca plants, the natives were also very fond of oak trees. They liked it so much that they began to purposely plant oak trees down one particular valley. Not only did oak have sturdy wood for things like bows, but its acorns could be picked during the fall.

They would usually pick more food than was needed for the day. They stored the excess grains in large baskets made of yucca fibers, raised from the ground to protect them from being eaten by bugs and other critters. To give thanks for the abundance of food, they often held festivals of endless storytelling, feasts, dancing, and sometimes even magic tricks. Some of these festivals lasted for many days.

Every night, they could look up into the sky and from the mountains to the coast; they could clearly see a thick milky white band of stars hanging above their heads in majestic wonder. They called this band of stars, "Hatotkeur". The elders would draw the patterns of the sky into the dirt and use the picture to explain to children and young adults where they fit in the universe and what was expected of them from their village.

They used hand held rocks called "manos" to dig holes into larger rocks called "mortars", originally to catch rainwater until about 7000 BCE, when people north of the Drying Out Place learned that they can also grind and mix food with the same rocks. They would collect sea shells of various sizes, and use large ones for bowls and smaller ones as spoons. One type of food they learned to make was named "sha-wee". To make this, the women would go and collect acorns from the oak trees that grew around the area during the fall. If they managed to pick a lot of acorns that day, the men would help with heavy lifting, but otherwise, the women did much of the gathering. Using a manos and mortar, they would grind the acorns into a fine dust, and after washing it in warm or sometimes boiling water, they would let it dry on leaves, and either eat it like so, or make a variety of other foods with it, including bread.

The La-Jolla Complex

The paleo-indians who migrated to San Diego developed a culture called the La Jollans. They became astronomers: As humans were pattern seekers, the natives would follow the patterns of the stars and planets as they danced crossed the sky and used them to track the time of day, year, seasons, and festivals. They did this by collecting pumus and basalt rocks and placing them in certain positions that would line them up with events like solstices and the equinoxes.

There was a third set of rocks that marked what is believed to be the agave season in mid-March. The agave plant was the first to come into season during that time, so it may have marked a whole season worth of desert harvesting. The constellations that the ancient Greeks and Romans noticed and named were the same ones that the natives of San Diego noticed, but the names were different. The Orion Constellation was called "Stretched Out Beaver Skin" because it looked like Orion's arm was stretched out and was holding what looks like skin. A group of stars called the Pleiades was named, "They Are Dancing", and Venus, the morning and evening star, once believed to be two different stars that could be seen brightly before the sun rose and set, was called "It Brings The Day" and "It Brings The Night".

During the winters, they would live further inland in the desert where it was warmer and gather muskete beans, barrel cacti and guajava plants. The villages on the coast would have relatives living among the villages in the desert, which probably led to many winter festivals. Come spring, they would move back to the shore and collect mollusks. The ones that stayed in the desert during the summer would dig fish traps along the shore line of Lake Cahuilla that would capture fish coming to shallow waters to lay their eggs.

Barrel cauctus would have its pricks removed and used as fish hooks while carving the rest of the plant up like pineapple. Desert lilies were treated as onions are. The fruits of guajava plants could be ground up like acorns. They would also harvest buckwheat seeds to grind and turn into a type of flower. The red fruit that grows on holly leaf cherries in the fall can be eaten like normal cherries, but the seeds inside can also be ground up. The roots of cattails could taste like cucumber. Manzanita berries were also harvested for food and medicine. in the fall, pinyon nuts from pinyon pines would also be harvested.

They were traders: Seeing as they hunted and gathered, surpluses were important. A great way to gain a surplus, or a variety of different things, was to trade with other bands and tribes. Villages from the coast would trade back and forth with villages from the mountains and deserts. They established routes for travel, trade and as a means of communication with each other, many of these routes would someday become roads or highways. One of their main trade routes went from the coast, up the Drying Out Place, towards the east, which later became part of Interstate 8 (also known as Kumeyaay highway). They would trade various goods, such as fish, abalone, seeds, acorns, tobacco, eagle feathers, and information.

They were warriors: Their main tools were bows and arrows made from oak trees, Mohave yuccas and agave leaves. Their arrows were in two parts, the arrowhead was attached to the front part which would fit into a back part. The back part is where the feathers would be attached and the part that would be retrieved after being fired. Throughout the reign of the natives, it's believed that long forsaken wars were fought by unremembered peoples. Many of their wars happened over people from one band, trespassing into the territory of another. There is no doubt there were battles and in their fury, the natives could be just as brave or ruthless, however one sees it, as any other human. There probably used to be great tales of epic Stone Aged battles between tribes and Homeric type warriors overcoming tremendous odds, earning the adulation of their peers and becoming immortalized in song and legend, retold over huge festivals: Stories that were important to those cultures and told to be remembered by future generations; stories that have since been lost in time. There are very little human remains from these times, for villages cremated their dead.

One of the ancient native stories is called, "How the Baron Long People came to be". It indicates that all of these bands used to be one large tribe that was on the move, migrating from the east, and following the sunset. But at the foot of a mountain in the Borrego desert, the Chief's daughter had a baby. That morning, the baby's father climbed the mountain and killed a deer to offer to the Chief. When he returned to offer the deer however, the Chief told the boy to cut it up and to give all the pieces away. They set up a large powwow or gathering that night where they all feasted on the deer and danced in celebration until the Chief announced that he was heartbroken by the birth of this baby and could go on no further. He instructed the rest of the tribe to move on without him, and then he then turned into stone. The tribe split up into bands, consisting of groups of families, and went their separate ways. One of the split factions continued to follow the sunset until they found their current home by the coast and settled there. Another story tells how all the bands once prepared for the coming of their god in the form of a serpent. They built a large round house, but it wasn't big enough so when the serpent god came and entered, the house caught fire and he was cremated. Not knowing what to do next, they held a council and determined that they must each eat a portion of the remains. But once they did, their language changed and they could no longer communicate with each other, and thus they went their separate ways until one faction ended up finding their current home by the coast and settling there. Kind of reminds me of a version of the tower of Babel tale.

These cycles were repeated for thousands and thousands of years. Their culture began to change at around 1000 BCE, when Yuman speaking people, migrated into the area and assimilated with the natives. It could have been those who brought the "How the Baron Long people came to be" story to the region. It is unknown whether the assimilation was peaceful or not though. What is known is that pottery and ceramics begin to be created and used for food storage, festivals and as the natives became more stationary and territorial; walls were raised for defense and irrigation, but it couldn't stop later generations from joining them. In 1000 CE, Shoshonean speaking people also migrated into the area. By this time, the cultures had settled into two distinct tribes: The "Ipai", which was a group of villages situated to the north of the Drying Out Place, and the "Tipai", a group of villages to the south of it. These tribes were further broken up into bands, which live as families in villages. Some of the Tipai bands included the villages of Otay to the south east of the foot of the bay, and Cosoy, again located in modern day Old Town and Presidio Park. Other villages included Chiap in modern day Chula Vista, Meti in modern day Spring Valley, Choyas located in a small valley south of Cosoy, Janat, Jamacha, Jamio, Onap, and Coapan, though there were many more scattered around the county.

Guacamals

They most likely learned of different humans living in other parts of the world from other natives along their trade routes just a few short years before, either that or by the first wave of diseases that spread from the south. There was no telling how the Ipai and Tipai initially thought of these other people, but seeing as news of wide spread death and devastation usually followed in the wake of contact between them and other villages, there was a good chance that they may have feared these mysterious white men who they referred to as "Guacamal". One day, fresh new rumors began to air from the trade routes to the east, possibly from a survivor. They told stories of white skinned men, wearing shiny and stylish clothes and holding lances and swords, pulling wagons and riding on the backs of large beasts the Spanish called "caballos". They are the descendants of the horses that managed to escape into Asia.

It is almost certain that the story talked of a large group of Guacamals coming from the south to a village somewhere beyond the mountains. The white men probably demanded the natives to supply them with food and other necessities, but then, for some reason, they began killing many of them. Once most of the village was slaughtered, the men simply gathered supplies and moved on. The survivors probably fled to the nearest villages for safety, telling their stories of horror and death, spreading fear into the hearts of villages all over the future United States.

Therefore, when it was rumored, that two large floating houses, which moved through the water by wind, were spotted in the waters to the south, many natives began to fear the worst. As the next day came and went, the two homes drifted closer and closer and became visible, passing the bare islands to the south and towards the mouth of the bay. Some Tipai who had been burning brush in the hunt for meat, saw the floating houses, put out the fires and began looking out into the coast in fear. The Ipai and Tipai had heard through the trade routes that this was how the deaths to the south and east began, with many of these wooden houses and rafts floating to the shore, or white men with strange clothing looking for supplies. The Tipai, the natives south of the Drying Out Place, probably had some heated debates amongst each other over how to handle the Guacamals if they arrived on shore. However, with very limited information of the actual situation or the resources to deter them from coming any further, they must have decided to wait and see if the men would come first.

The houses finally reached the mouth of the large bay to the south and stopped. Some of the Tipai carefully hid all throughout the coastline and watched the men, some no doubt armed. Natives from the top of the point that stuck out into the bay below the Drying Out Place could have probably peeked directly down and would have seen the movement of little people on the boxy floating houses bundling up the large skins that caught the wind and pushed them across the waters. They then may have witnessed a group of Guacamals sit in a large canoe and lower themselves into the water before lightly paddling to the shore toward a group of Tipai standing on the marshy beach. The natives might have also recognized their elaborate clothing and weapons from the stories passed along by other villages.By the time the small group of white men reached the shore however, the fears of many of the natives became so overwhelming that numbers of them ran off and hid, leaving only three of them to greet the strangers. The group of Guacamals reached the shore, exited the canoes, and carefully approached the remaining natives in an attempt to make first contact. I'm sure many thoughts ran through the minds of the future Kumeyaay who witnessed this event: I have a feeling that one of the things that went through their mind was: "It's true. These people really do exist."
Also "Why are they here?" "What were their intentions?"

"What's going to happen next?"

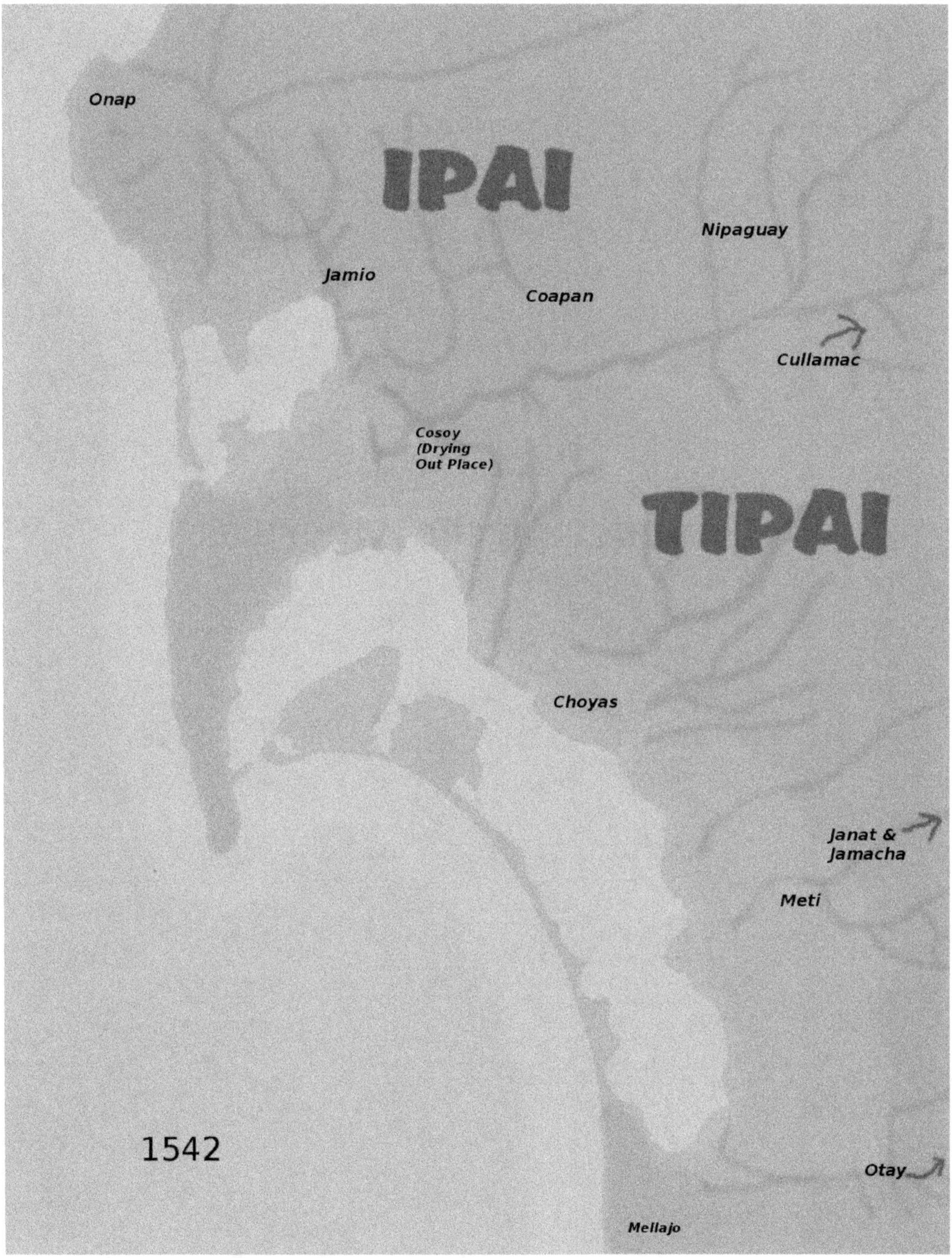

Fig. 7: San Diego Native Villages,
1542

Part Two:
Conquering the Americas

Four - Christopher Columbus

First Voyage

In the year 1492, Pope Alexander the Sixth ascended to the throne, the Torah was first printed on a press, and although the Castilian language had been around for a while, the first Castilian grammar book was published. Castilian is what Spanish was called before it was called Spanish. Since the Muslims took over Constantinople, Castile had found themselves competing with Portugal for alternative routes to Asia. At Palos de la Frontera, Spain, on the 3rd of August, a Genoan Admiral named Christopher Columbus led a fleet of three ships, the Nina, Pinta and Santa Maria, off on a voyage headed due west through the Ocean Sea (later called the Atlantic Ocean). Trusting the work of an astrologer named Paolo dal Pozzo Toscanelli, Columbus had greatly underestimated the size of the Earth and thought he had found an opportunity for riches. He wanted to reach Asia and establish trade there without having to go through the costly routes of the Middle East or around Africa. He was also going there to find gold.

After leaving shore, they headed southwest toward the Canary Islands, where Friar and someday Saint Diego of Alcala once spent many years as a missionary. Before arriving though, the rudder to one of Columbus' smaller ships, the Pinta, broke down. They spent the rest of the month repairing the ship and left again from the Canary Islands on September 6th, headed west. Nine days later, on the 15th, Columbus' journal read:

"...in the early part of the night there fell from heaven into the

sea a marvelous flame of fire…"

This author can only think of two things they could have seen. It could have been either a lightning bolt, or a meteorite. Being stuck in a hot wooden ship in the middle of the ocean and super-religious, I'm sure witnessing this marvelous but sudden flame of fire was probably seen by the crew as a bad omen.

Columbus was afraid that if his crew knew the true distance they were traveling, the crew would mutiny, so he did two things to keep them calm. First, he would lie about the distance they had traveled day to day. For example, the next day, on the 16th, Columbus estimated they had traveled thirty nine leagues. He would record that distance in his personal journal, but in a second journal meant for the crew, he recorded the distance traveled that day as thirty six leagues. For the 17th, they traveled fifty leagues, but Columbus recorded forty seven. This would continue until they found actual land.

The other thing he would do is highlight almost any sort of activity as signs that they were near land. Clouds, floating weeds, sea life, and birds flying overhead were all signs "of the proximity of land". On the 19th, two birds recorded as "boobies" arrived at the fleet of ships (they were actually Albatross' but after a month at sea, Columbus and his men must have had other things in mind). These "boobies" excited Columbus who claimed to his crew that these types of birds don't generally travel over twenty leagues away from land.

After a hundred and eight more leagues and many more spotted "boobies", the captain of the Pinta, called that he had seen land. The crew from the Nina, then climbed the masts of their ship and confirmed what was seen. Everybody celebrated and altered course southwest, but after a day of traveling, they found that what they had seen were only distant or low clouds. They had come to believe that they had passed some islands following the clouds. Realizing that they had been out at sea much longer than anticipated, the crew began to speak of mutiny. They wanted to turn around and either head back to one of these islands, or back to Castile, fearing they would die at sea if they did not. Some of them plotted to throw the Admiral overboard.

Columbus continued with his course, lying about how much they had traveled and declaring everything that floats or flies as a sign of impending land. There was a reward from the Crown for the first person to spot land so the crew was alert. On the morning of October 7th, the Nina rode out ahead and claimed they had seen land. The other ships joined, but because of the haze, waited until the evening to look for what was seen, but I guess there was no land. They kept going for three more days before the Captains of the other ships confronted Columbus, telling their Admiral that they would go on for only three more days. In regards to Columbus' reaction, the journal for October 10th states:

"But the Admiral cheered them up in the best way he could, giving them good hopes of the advantages they might gain from it. He added that, however much they might complain, he had to

go to the Indies, and that he would go on until he found them, with the help of our Lord."

This apparently pacified his men for now, but Columbus' time was running out.

On the morning of the 12th, the Moon rose from the east at its third quarter. The crew of the Pinta, sailed ahead to look for land. A crew member named Rodrigo de Triana spotted a sandy island illuminated by the moonlight. A flag was raised and a gun was fired. Cries of "Terra, Terra!" rang. This time it was for real: They had indeed found land. They arrived at the island that morning and first observation they made was of all the naked people who called the island "Guanahani". The Christians brought out all of their flags and swords, gifts and gods at landing. They went on shore and performed a little ceremony on the beach, where they claimed the island in the name of the Castilian Crown and renamed it "San Salvador".

There is no telling what was going through the minds of the natives of Guanahani, now San Salvador, who witnessed this ceremony. In a letter he later wrote to Luis de Santiangel, Columbus boasts that he took possession of the island in front of witnesses, native and otherwise, "and I was not gainsaid (challenged)", despite the fact that he knew the natives didn't speak Castilian and so had no idea he was usurping their territory for a crown of a distant land. After claiming the land, the Christians and the natives met for the first time and the Christians greeted them with small gifts, such as glass beads.

Columbus treated these gifts like throw away items, as he highlighted how cheap they were in his journals. Seemingly relieved, the natives who called themselves the "Taino", came over to the enormous ships, bringing gifts of their own. Still thinking that they had landed in the East Indies, Columbus mistakenly referred to the natives in the region as "indios". Today the word is "indian".

In the closest surviving thing to his journal, which is actually a third hand account, Columbus speculated that the Indians of the region would make great servants and could easily be converted into Christians. He saw some wounds on a few natives and asked them how they got them. They told him that they had a battle with people from a nearby island. He noticed a lack of metal weapons, and when he showed them a sword, they grabbed it by the blade end, accidentally cutting their hand in the process. He also noted:

"It appeared to me to be a race of people very poor in everything...They have no iron, their darts being wands without iron... They should be good servants and intelligent, for I observed that they quickly took in what was said to them, and I believe that they would easily be made Christians, as it appeared to me that they had no religion... I, our Lord being pleased, will take hence, at the time of my departure, six natives for your Highnesses, that they may learn to speak."

It appears he actually took about three that day, and one even had to be carried off by force, though this is not mentioned in the journal until days later. The Christians and their native captives returned to the ship that night with canoes arriving at the ship the next day. According to the log, there was a trading extravaganza at the ship as cotton and skins were traded for caps and beads. However, neither Columbus nor his men were looking for skins. They were looking for gold, and like a detective, he picked up on the clues. He noticed a few small gold nuggets attached to the noses of some of the natives and asked the Taino where they got them. He learned of a king to the south who had cups full of these pieces. He tried to get them to lead him to this king, thinking it might be the Khan in Marco Polo's book, but the natives weren't interested in taking him.

Their arrival well known to the Indians now, the Christians continued to sail on the 14th. All along the shore as they followed the coast, natives would come to the shore, bearing gifts and begging them to come to shore. Some natives believed they had come from heaven, as Columbus and his men understood it. In his journal, the Admiral reiterates the inferiority of the Indians:

"…(T)hese people are very simple as regards the use of arms, as your Highnesses will see from the seven that I caused to be taken, to bring home and learn our language and return; unless your Highness should order them all to be brought to Castile, or to be kept as captives on the same island; for with fifty men they can all be subjugated and made to do what is required of them…

The natives make war on each other, although these are very simple-minded and handsomely-formed people."

Just one day before, he was hoping to pick up six natives, unless there is a mistranslation in the journal, now it seems he wants seven. A canoe followed the Nina that night and seeing his chance, one of the native captives jumped ship and swam to the canoe, where it then sped away. The next day, Columbus continued on his voyage, landing on another island he named "Santa Maria de la Concepcion".

"For the people I had taken from the island of San Salvador told me that here they wore very large rings of gold on their arms and legs."

On the way, a second canoe pulled up, prompting another Indian to jump ship and escape. When the third canoe arrived with a man wishing to trade cotton, they took no chances and told him to climb aboard. When he didn't, a few men jumped in and seized him and his canoe by force. He was brought to Columbus, where he gave the man some beads, bells, and a cap. Seeing that he was just looking to trade, Columbus then ordered the native's canoe returned to him and for his men to let him go with his gifts and his cotton. Then, he decided to let the remaining native go. It is here when his journal just happened to mention that they had forcefully carried that one away before.

His mercy was for appearances though, because he bragged in his journal about how he got the natives to see them as good people in hopes that they would be friendly to him when he returned. Before the voyage had started, he had already negotiated the governorship of any land he found, so all he needed was to find a source of gold and he could become a very rich man. As he hopped from island to island, he picked up more natives.

Next, he headed for a really long island that he called "Fernandina". Here, Columbus' journal notes a native who bartered in dried leaves that he found valuable, possibly tobacco! The man was taken on board, fed, given gifts and released to win his favor. Columbus continued to circle islands and trading with the natives. Most of his journal entry for October 17th, talks of the interesting wild life and how similar, yet different they are to the wild life in Castile. When he saw a man with an especially large piece of gold on his nose, Columbus mistook it for a form of currency and in his words, "quarreled with these people because they would not exchange or give what was required", whatever that means.

On October 23, he set out for an island that the Indians called "Cuba", which since he thought he was in the West Indies, thought it might be where the island of "Cipango"(Japan) was. He made it there on the 28th and was amazed at the plant life and natural harbors of the island. He would later state that the island was bigger than England and Scotland combined, which was not true at all. He was still looking for this king with cups full of gold, or at least a gold mine, but couldn't find them there.

He named the island "La Isla Juana".

While on another island on November 12th, Columbus relays the following sadness:

"Yesterday a canoe came alongside the ship, with six youths in it. Five came on board, and I ordered them to be detained. They are here now. I afterwards sent to a house on the western side of the river, and seized seven women, old and young, and three children. I did this because the men would behave better in Spain if they had women of their own land, than without them... The same night, the husband of one of the women came alongside in a canoe, who was father of the three children... He asked me to let him come with them...They are now all consoled at being with one who is a relation of them all."

I thought he only wanted six or seven natives, but I guess sixteen is close enough.

To calm the captives, they were led to believe that they would be released once the Christians found gold. Two youths escaped the Nina five days later. While exploring, Columbus would also have his men cut down trees to make large crosses out of them and leave them on each island.

On December 5th he landed on Hispaniola, which now holds Haiti and the Dominican Republic. He described the landscape as a marvel and spoke about how the rivers and streams carried gold. He left some men behind, but took more natives. He found an island full of turtles and named it "Tortuga"(aww).

On December 17th, near the Island of Tortuga, he finally got a real taste of what he was looking for.

"They saw one man... with a piece of gold leaf as large as a hand, and it appears that he wanted to barter with it. He cut the leaf into small pieces, and each time he came out he brought a piece and exchanged it. When he had no more left, he said by signs that he had sent for more, and that he would bring it another day."

Later that day, a group of Indians from Tortuga arrived, but the man with the gold leaf berated the group and sent them away, throwing rocks at their canoe as they left and encouraging the Spaniards to join in. The next day, they met with the king of the Indians that were from the Island of Hispaniola. After referring to their nakedness for about the fiftieth time, Columbus had dinner, exchanged gifts and became quick friends with these natives. That night, with their help, the Spanish erected a wooden cross on the Island.

They found a large port of another island they dubbed Santo Tomas on December 20th. Columbus was once again awe-struck by its natural beauty. The next day he and his men went on shore and did their usual gift exchanges. They sent a few Christians to check out their villages and he spent a few pages describing it all. This happened again on the 22nd and by the 23rd, his ships were surrounded by over a hundred curious canoes.

They spent Christmas day (December 25th) navigating the waters. With the waters calm that night, Columbus went to bed on his flagship, the Santa Maria. With the night so calm, the journal claims that "the sailor who steered the ship thought he would go to sleep, leaving the tiller in (the) charge of a boy". While they slept, the water current took the Santa Maria and gently beached it on a sandbank and the damaged ship began to take in a rush of sea water. Though the beaching was hardly felt, Columbus quickly awoke and went to work trying to save his ship, but to no avail. He had tried to get some of his men to take a boat out to lay an anchor towards the sea, but they instead took a boat and tried to seek refuge on one of the other ships.

Columbus was lucky to have made friends with the Natives of that island, who helped him unload his old ship, for it saved him and his men a lot of time, and staying there gave them great insights in their quest for gold. From then on, Columbus would finish his voyage on the Nina. Finally finding a gold source, he orders a fort to be built with the intention of leaving a few men behind, under the protection of the local king there.

On January 4th, Columbus and his ships departed the island, but it seems as though there was some drama between him and his men which actually delayed their trip back east a few more days. They finally got underway on January 16th and made it back home on March 13, 1493. When Columbus returned to Castile, with the natives and other treasure, he was sure that he had found a new path to the Indies and thus had immortalized himself in history. Columbus returned a hero.

Indeed, he was immortalized, but not for reaching the east coast of Asia. When word had gone out that a western path to the Indies had been established, Pope Alexander VI released the "Discovery Doctrine". It decreed that lands void of Christians was available for discovery. Also, all "discovered" land east of the new lands be given to Portugal, which will give them a sizable chunk of land as well. Either way, the Castilian Crown was given full authority of any lands found west of the islands, including the authority over non-Christians in the hopes of converting them. This opened the door for a new age of "discoverers" called the "Conquistadors".

In the end, Columbus did seem to actually discover something that nobody knew about before. Those were the trade winds that blew him across the expanse of the Ocean Sea and back. It would send many more people across the ocean from here on.

Other Voyages

Before his second voyage in 1493, Columbus sent a letter to Ferdinand and Isabella with ideas on how he planned on running the Islands. He asked for two thousand settlers to join him and suggested setting up about four colonies on Hispaniola with a mayor and a clerk. He also asked for priests or friars to come and build churches and convert the natives in the island into Christianity. He adds that nobody should look for gold without permission and what gold that is found will be melted down and stamped with a seal. He then goes into details on how to divide said gold.

As a side note, a letter from the Crown to their secretary, Fernando de Zafra dated May 23, 1493, told him to collect twenty horseman and horses from Granada and to take them to Seville by June 20th.

Columbus got most of what he asked for and on September 24, 1493, he set sail a second time, now with seventeen ships and two thousand settlers. On the way, they encountered and survived their first hurricane. He further explored the inhabited islands he had previously "discovered", but this time, he wouldn't be so nice to the natives. Thinking Cuba could now be a peninsula in the Chinese mainland, he further explored it and Jamaica, finding another island called "Burenquen", the future island of Puerto Rico.

When he landed on his first inhabited island, the natives fled their dwellings. On their first Voyage, Columbus ordered his men to leave the huts alone and to take nothing. This time he and his men took all sorts of stuff from the small huts. However, they also found lots of human bones and limbs in the area. I'm assuming this helped to shape the settlers initial views of the natives. On visits to other islands, they took prisoners. One group of natives, while on the boat back to the ship, decided to attack their captives, wounding one of them, but to no avail. The wounded man and a "mortally wounded" native also died.

On November 22, he set anchor at Hispaniola and began looking for the men that he left from the first voyage. They were supposed to set up the first colony, La Navidad. Columbus first met with the king on the island, who had offered the men in the colony protection. He asked the King about his men who told him that some "had died from disease, and the others had been killed in quarrels that had arisen amongst them". Then when he found the settlement, he learned that the fort he had built on the first voyage had been burnt down and that all of his men had been killed. The natives claimed that the Spaniards had taken their women and that "they had been killed by Caonabo and Mayreni" - two native tribal leaders.

He then set up a new settlement called La Isabela, but chose a poor location. Then some more sadness with the natives:

"They all say they wish to be Christians, although in truth they're idolaters, for in their houses they have many kinds of figures; when asked what such a figure was, they would reply that it is a thing of Turey, by which they meant "of Heaven." I made a pretense of throwing them on the fire, which grieved them so that they began to weep."

Eventually they do find the gold they are looking for, but they realize they have to dig for it. Sadly, we all know who is going to do the digging.

Among other things, the first horses to walk on the Americas in thousands of years, first walked on November 28, 1493. The natives were in awe of them, but afraid because they thought that they might eat humans.

Columbus returned to Hispaniola on August 20th to govern. As governor, he occupied the island, enslaved the native population within those islands and allowed settlers to use them as labor to mine gold and set up some new colonies. To note how bad it got for the natives of the region, a friend of Columbus who went with him wrote the following regarding a "gift" he was given:

"While I was in the boat, I captured a very beautiful Carib woman, whom the said Lord Admiral (Columbus) gave to me. When I had taken her to my cabin she was naked as was their custom. I was filled with a desire to take my pleasure with her and attempted to satisfy my desire. She was unwilling, and so treated me with her nails that I wished I had never begun. But— to cut a long story short—I then took a piece of rope and whipped her soundly, and she let forth such incredible screams that you would not have believed your ears. Eventually we came to such terms, I assure you, that you would have thought that she had been brought up in a school for whores."

It is hard to read some of these accounts at times. It is sometimes even hard to keep an objective mind about it, so let me take this time to say; fuck that dude. However, the truth is that the island's inhabitants were not all a peaceful people: they were at war with each other before Columbus ever arrived, would often do pillaging of their own, and when Columbus came for them, could never put away their differences and unify against him. A letter from the ship's physician Dr. Chanca says:

"The habits of these Caribbees are brutal... all these are alike as

if they were of one race, who do no injury to each other; but each and all of them wage war against the other neighboring islands... In their attacks upon the neighboring islands, these people capture as many of the woman as they can, especially those who are young and beautiful, and keep them for servants and to have as concubines; and so great a number do they carry off, that in fifty houses no men were to be seen; and out of the number of the captives, more than twenty were young girls. These women also say that the Caribbees use them with such cruelty as would scarcely be believed; and that they eat the children which they bear to them, and only bring up those which they have by their native wives."

So really, these were warring cultures who had been conqured by a more powerful warring culture, not mearly peaceful people invaded by outsiders. Though to be fair, those details are highly disputed.

Columbus did some more exploring, still trying to find China and Japan. He was so convinced that Cuba was part of the Chinese mainland, that he had anyone who suggested that it was an island whipped. He sent a letter to Isabella asking to enslave a population of Caribbees, but the Queen decided against it. Despite the Queen's objection, the free work the natives produced began to return profits, so she was ignored.

As Governor, Columbus eventually established a tribute system. Every native above the age of fourteen had to pay the Spaniards a certain amount of gold every three months. In exchange for the gold, they received a copper token. They had to wear this token around their necks. If they were caught without one, their hands would be cut off and they would be allowed to bleed to death. Many of the natives, up to fifty thousand according to Columbus, soon began to commit suicide rather than to be tortured, mutilated or violated.

On August 20, 1494, Columbus returned to Spain.
Four years after Columbus' second voyage, rumors began to brew of a whole continent laying southwest of the Cape Verde Islands. These rumors spurred a third Columbus voyage in 1498.

This voyage was both a resupply mission and an exploration through the islands in search of the Asia mainland. It was also another gold hunting trip. Six ships left, with three going to Hispaniola to resupply the island and the other three, Columbus included, traveling to the Canaries, then to the Cape Verde Islands, then southwest until July 31, 1498, when he landed on the Island of Trinidad.

Columbus did eventually reach the continent, but it was the South American mainland of Venezuela where he met the Maya, who had begun to re-emerge. He believed he had landed on a continent south of the Chinese mainland however. His health was beginning to fail him, he had bad arthritis, and signs point to him slowly losing his mind, yet on August 12th Columbus set sail for Hispaniola. He arrived on the 19th to angry colonists who then began to rebel against his leadership. He and his brothers responded with an iron fist, allowing people to starve and apparently even had some of his own crew hanged. There were no trials. The punishment for a Christian boy that was caught stealing grain was to have his ears and nose cut off before auctioning him off as a slave.

Yes, sadly, Christians did that stuff too. It was even worse for the Indians. Even though Columbus initially intended on converting the natives, that would mean they couldn't become slaves and by then, their work on the colonies had become so necessary that he began to deny baptisms to them so they could be auctioned as slaves.

By October 1499, after a year of cruelty, Columbus wore himself out and sent two ships to Spain to ask for a royal commissioner to assist him in governing. This was a mistake. With the ship, went angry colonists and their native wives... or slaves, as well as frustrated missionaries and stories of the cruelties in the West Indies. The Crown, angry that Columbus disobeyed her orders with such barbarity, appointed Francisco de Bobadilla to replace Columbus as governor. Bobadilla arrived at Hispaniola in August 23, 1500, and received enough complaints and testimony to arrest Columbus and his brothers and send them back to Spain in chains.

Upon returning to Spain, Columbus and his brothers were jailed for six weeks. Afterwards, the crown summoned them and he was tried for mismanagement, but not for his cruelties. He lost his titles and his standing, but convinced the Crown to allow him one last voyage. Meanwhile, Governor Bobadilla died in

1502 and was replaced by Nicolas de Ovando y Caceres, who also hated Columbus.

Columbus' last voyage began in May 12, 1502 and had him searching for the Strait of Malacca, which is actually located in the Java Sea, on the other side of the world, but still believing he had found a passage to Asia, Columbus thought it was nearby, confusing the Caribbean for the Java Sea. He had made a lot of promises to the Crown and knew that he had to deliver, but he was otherwise a ruined man. He tried to sail under the Bahamas and around the mainland, but ended up blocked by the Mayan coastline. He sailed south down the coast line for two months before he met with people called the Ngobe who told him of where to find gold. They also told him that there was another ocean just beyond the western mountains, but he chose not to look for it. Instead, he chose to start problems with the indigenous by setting up a fort at the mouth of the Belen River after being told not to do so.

And of course, he and his men kidnapped the native chief who told them not to explore the Belen. That guy escaped, came back with an army and repelled the Christians off the future lands of Panama. Columbus and his men quickly returned to their ships to set sail, but the natives came and attacked the ships and many had to be abandoned. Columbus intended to make it to Hispaniola, but on the way, they encountered a hurricane and so instead became shipwrecked and stranded in Jamaica. The new governor of Hispaniola refused to help him when he learned of Columbus' misfortune, so he spent the next year stranded in

Jamaica, with his health declining.

The only reason he survived through that year was because he was able to horrify the natives there by successfully predicting a lunar eclipse. Throughout history, a lunar eclipse was thought to be a sign of bad luck and so he decided to take advantage of that knowledge. On February 29, 1503, he gathered the natives, told them they had been wicked and the spirits would punish them by turning the moon blood red - and just like he said, the moon turned red. Now terrified and believing Columbus had somehow caused the eclipse, the natives treated him well.

After being stranded for a year, the Governor finally sent some relief and Columbus was sent back to Castile, thus concluding his voyages.

Columbus would die on May 20, 1506, still believing he had reached Asia.

Five - First American Adventures

Mapping and Naming the Americas

While Columbus was doing all that terrible shit, more people began to sail west, thinking they were headed to Asia. An Italian cartographer and explorer named Amerigo Vespucci, on his third voyage to what many then believed was Asia, wrote in 1502 that the Asian land mass on maps was very different from what he had just visited, meaning that the place may not be Asia after all, but a whole new continent. This became big news back in Spain, where in 1504, inspired by tales of treasures, women, and empire in what people were beginning to call the New World, a man named Hernan Cortez left his hometown in Spain and sailed to Hispaniola, looking for adventure, we'll get into his antics on the following chapter.

By 1507, new maps had been updated to include what they believed the new continents might look like. In honor of Vespucci's light bulb moment, a German cartographer named Martin Waldseemuller in his updated world map book gave the continent the name of "America", believing it was Vespucci who had "discovered" it and not Columbus. Though the maps were still inaccurate at this time, it allowed future explorers a guide in which to travel.

Though it was big news, the "discovery" of the Americas still wasn't good news. This meant the western path to Asia was blocked by these large landmasses stretching from north to south. To make it worse, they had no idea how large the continents were. At first, attempts were made to sail around the southern tip of the continents, but it was shown that the voyage would be way too long to be practicable. Explorers then decided to see if they could find a passage through it, since there was a skinny sliver of land in the middle. This led to the belief that somewhere on one of the continents was a water route that led straight from the Atlantic, to Asia.

Queen Califia

In around 1510, a Spanish writer, man named Garci Rodríguez de Montalvo wrote a romance novel named "Las sergas de Esplandián" or "The Exploits of Esplandian". It was the fifth book in a series of popular books called "Amadis of Gaul", and is sort of a take on the Crusades. This specific story seems to be a side story in the series. The story featured a large but beautiful black woman named Califia, a take on the Arabic word "khalifa" meaning leader, who ruled over a kingdom of cave dwelling amazon women from a mythical island that went by the name of "California". The Island was situated east of the Java Sea (the sea Columbus had actually been looking for) and was full of steep cliffs, rocky shores and creatures called griffins. These griffins ate only one thing: Men. It was fabled that gold was the only metal found there, and that it was used to make everything from jewelry to harnesses. Califia and her kingdom of amazon women were great warriors, but knew nothing of Christianity, or Islam, or about any other religion of the outside world: They were pagans. In order to stay wealthy and to fulfill her zeal for exploration, Califia had many fleets of ships built and would set up expeditions to plunder surrounding areas. Any man who stood in their way, they fed to the griffins.

In one of her expeditions, she ends up in Constantinople and meets a Muslim warrior, named Radiaro. Califia agreed to help Radiaro and the Muslims take Constantinople from the Christians without really knowing which side stood for what. Confident of her skills either way, she tells him to sit back and let her do her work.

During the siege, she releases the griffins, but rather than eat or kill all of the Christian men, they simply ate any man, regardless of religion. After realizing that many Muslims were also being killed, Califia pulled back her griffins and engaged the enemy hand to hand. While fighting, she hears of a very handsome man - I guess all of the fighting must have bored her. She then meets the Christian Esplandian and falls in love with him at first sight. Love stricken, she loses the will to fight, and gives up her war, admitting that her pagan faith was inadequate to fight against the Christian faith and pledges allegiance to it. She and her people were then baptized as Christians and I would guess... married off? She married one of Esplandian's relatives, since he was already set to marry another woman. Califia seemed to have no issue with being passed down, and returned with her new husband to the island of California to rule it as a Christian nation. The end. Fin. Blackout. Applause.

It was a side story to the main plot of the novels, but it became a very popular book. It wasn't long before people began to believe that such an island full of women and gold may indeed exist, and some soon began to search for this mysterious island of California... or maybe not. Maybe the way the name from this novel became attached to the land was through a mark of sarcasm... You will be filled in on that later in the book.

Vasco Núñez de Balboa

On Columbus' second voyage, he brought Rodrigo de Bastidas with him. When Bastidas returned to Spain, he petitioned the Crown for his own voyage and in 1499, permission was granted. In his voyage, he traveled to South America and is sometimes credited as the "discoverer" of a thin strip of land that connected the Americas, later known as the Isthmus of Panama, despite the fact that Columbus had landed there during his fourth voyage... and in spite of the native people already living there. During that voyage however, Bastidas' leaky ships forced them to trade their way back to Hispaniola. He brought the former captain of the Santa Maria, Juan de la Cosa, and a Spanish man named Vasco Núñez de Balboa with him. Balboa traveled up and down the American coast for a few years gaining experience and knowledge of the area during this time.

Meanwhile, Vasco de Gama was the real first explorer to reach India via the ocean. He also left for a second voyage to start a factory in Calicut. Pedro Alvarez Cabral reached modern day Brazil in South America from Portugal before crossing back over the Atlantic, around South Africa, and landing in India. Once they had set a foothold into India, they sent Francisco de Almeida in 1505 to take control of the Spice trade in India. Almeida then became its Viceroy.

Back in Hispaniola, Balboa had returned from his voyages rich but had soon gone into debt. He decided to stow away on a ship, hiding in a barrel, to get away from his debtors... because back then, it really wasn't that easy to get away from creditors! The ship soon departed, headed for the South American mainland. Balboa was eventually discovered, but since he knew a lot about the area, they decided to put him to use. A colony called "San Sebastian" was established, but was destroyed by natives in the region who probably remembered that one time when Columbus came and set up a post where he weren't supposed to and kidnapped their King. Balboa suggested a new site for a camp and so they moved to the site and fought the natives there, enriching themselves in the process, and in 1510, Santa Maria la Antigua del Darién was established by Balboa, and was the first permanent Spanish colony in the American mainland.

In 1511, it was decided that the island of Cuba would be invaded from Hispaniola. A man named Diego Velázquez de Cuéllar was sent to keep order and become the Island's governor. To prepare, he asked his buddy Pánfilo de Narváez for thirty crossbowmen. Narvaez recruited a man named Juan Rodriguez Cabrillo as an assistant, but his skills on the crossbow impressed Narvaez, who would bring him on a future voyage.

Meanwhile in 1513, while exploring more of the Caribbean Sea, Ponce de Leon "discovered" what he believed was an island. After seeing its bright, flowery landscape, he named it, "La Florida". The same year Florida was being "discovered", Vasco Núñez de Balboa, now a well-liked and successful governor, successfully crossed over the mountains in the isthmus of Central America. These mountains were the same ones Columbus declined to cross in his fourth voyage, making Balboa the first European to behold the ocean on the other side. He called it, "Mar del Sur", or the South Sea. They soon founded a city on the west coast of the Isthmus named Nuestra Señora de la Asunción de Panamá, or Our Lady of the Assumption of Panama. The word Panama does not mean "PAN-AMericA", which this author had originally believed, but was thought to be named after a Native American fishing village that sat where the ruins of Panama Viejo now are. In this village, the native word "panama" meant "many fish".

Finding riches in the Darién and in Panama, Balboa sent ships from Panama full of the Crown's share of the treasures to Hispaniola in the year 1511. Once again, a hurricane caused the ships to wreck off the coast of Jamaica. Fifteen men survived making it to the Yucatán Peninsula on lifeboats where they were captured by the Maya. All but two died in the hands of the Maya: Geronimo de Agular, and Gonzalo Gurrero.

After Balboa confirmed the Isthmus to be narrow enough to pass to the South Sea, it became a major crossroad for Spain's expanding empire. Ships would anchor off the east, travel from the Darién to Panama by land, and from there, sail either up and down the coast, or across the ocean. For a while, the route was known as "Camino de Cruces", or "Road of the Crosses", because of the grave sites one would pass as they walked through the dangerous and mosquito infested land. By 1538, the isthmus and old city would become part of the Viceroyalty of Peru.

Quetzalcoatl

Quetzalcoatl means, "Feathered serpent" in Nahuatl, which is the ancient language of the Mexicas. However, it is also the name of a god who was born to a virgin named Chimalman. There are many variations of his story, but according to the myths, the Mexicas, later known to the rest of the world as the Aztecs, believed that time was cyclical, not linear, that there had been four previous suns and worlds, which had all been destroyed. From his own blood and the bones of the dead, Quetzalcoatl created humans and the fifth sun from the location of an ancient city named Teotihuacan. He then taught the humans in the area how to plant maize (corn), write and tell time. It is unclear if he was for or against human sacrifice. After becoming drunk and sleeping with a priestess, Quetzalcoatl felt bad and burned himself to death, which I have no choice but to conclude was an overreaction. His heart rose to the sky, glowing brighter and brighter, eventually becoming the morning star.

With the collision of the Spanish and Native American cultures, came the first truly global trade, which included an exchange of crops, animals, people, and diseases. The old world, represented by Afro-Eurasia, had never experienced the marvels of corn, potatoes, tomatoes, pumpkins, turkeys, toucans, lamas, coffee beans, cocoa beans, or syphilis before the Columbus expedition. At the same time, the new world represented by the Americas, had never heard of oranges, horses, cattle, pigs, chickens, cats, smallpox, measles, the bubonic plague or Christianity. The biodiversity of both worlds changed so much after Columbus that the diets and populations of humanity would never be the same again. The old world could now make proto-pizzas and whatever led up to the new world creation of KFC could now begin. In addition, so many Natives would later die of diseases that entire cities were abandoned and in time, forests regrew over them. With more jungle and forests in South America, CO_2 levels dropped worldwide. This made the year 1492 a candidate for the beginning of a completely new epoch called the Anthropocene, but it lost to the year 1950.

Six – Hernan Cortez
1517 - 1519

In the ancient city of Tenochtitlan, Moctezuma the Second sat in his bath overlooking his land and went into thought. He was beginning to notice strange things happening in his growing kingdom and it had begun to worry him. A few years ago, a column of fire appeared at night and when the Sun rose the next morning, the light was blocked by the smoke and the fire that had rained back down. Since then, seven other omens captured his concern. Various temples had spontaneously caught fire or had been hit by lightning and had been destroyed. A comet had broken through the sky and exploded into three pieces in broad daylight and recently, on a bird's head, he had seen a pattern representing the stars of Mamalhuatztli, which gave him a scary vision. Though he asked his soothsayers what these signs may have meant, nobody knew.

Moctezuma, now feeling clean but still preoccupied, left his bath and went on with his afternoon.

In Spanish occupied Cuba during the year 1517, the same year as the "column of fire", Governor Velázquez commissioned a fleet to the Yucatán peninsula. They met the Maya there, who eventually slaughtered most of the crew. The survivors returned to Cuba in 1518 and told the Governor what they saw. One of these men named Juan de Grijalva said that he had reached the mainland and learned that the area contained lots and lots of gold. Now interested, Velázquez decided to send another fleet.

Hernan Cortez was put under command of the expedition. He was given six hundred men and eleven ships to explore the inner region of South America and ready it for colonization. He was not authorized to conquer anything, but Cortez, a legal scholar who had become bored with his daytime job, had different plans. By 1519, his friend and Cuban Governor Diego Velázquez de Cuéllar, who was the one who picked him for the voyage in the first place, decided to revoke his commission, on behalf of some personal issues involving some of Velázquez's sisters who Cortez had relations with. Never-the-less Cortez, the stubborn player he was, had invested a considerable amount of his own wealth into this fleet though, so he had his replacement ambushed and killed, then went ahead with the expedition anyways, infuriating Velázquez, who decided to send yet another fleet to find and return Cortez to Cuba.

The trip was short. As soon as Cortez's fleet landed in the Yucatán, they met up with the native Maya, who also tried to slaughter them, but every time the Spaniards were ambushed, they were able to successfully defeat the Mayan forces. In an apparent peace agreement, the Maya gave the Spanish five native women. One of these women, named Malintzin, was a multilingual Maya princess who was sold into slavery by her royal parents. She could speak Nahuatl, the language of the Aztecs, as well as her native Mayan. This would have gave Cortez a translator... but she didn't know Spanish at the time. Lucky for Cortez though, he had previously found Geronimo de Aguilar, who had been previously shipwrecked. He had been on the Yucatan for so long, he had taken a Mayan wife and had learned their language. Through these two, Cortez will be able to communicate with the Aztecs.

There wasn't much gold where they were at, so they soon left. By April, 1519, he had sailed west to the other side on the Yucatan, out of Mayan territory and set up a camp. For legal reasons, he established the camp as a settlement, naming it La Villa Rica de la Vera Cruz (Veracruz). Before leaving the ships though, they received native visitors on canoes. The conversation between Cortez and these visitors is recorded in what is known as the Florentine Codex:

"They went on the pretext of seeking trade. So they went in disguise, to find out about them... [For] they had the opinion of the time that our Prince Quetzalcoatl had come.

The Spaniards called them, asked them: 'Who are you? From where have you come? Where is your home?'

At that moment they told them, 'We have come from México. Then they asked, 'If truly you are Mexicas, what is the name of the ruler of México?'

[They replied], 'Our lords, his name is Moctezuma.'"

This conversation may have extended to the point where Cortez asked Moctezuma's people, "Has your king any gold?", to which they answered, "Yes". He then gave the following brutally honest order:

"Let him send it to me, for I and my companions have a complaint - a disease of the heart, which only gold can cure."

Moctezuma later received word that his greeters had returned. When he met them, he heard their tale of the strange bearded men who came from the sea on floating mountains and rode on giant deer asking for gold. Since this was the year "One Reed", Moctezuma began to wonder if this had anything to do with the Quetzalcoatl prophecy or the recent omens. Intrigued or possibly frightened, he ordered for surveillance and sent a friendly delegation to greet the Spaniards.

Back in Veracruz, Cortez and the rest of the Spanish begin hearing stories too. From Cortez's first letter to the King of Spain:

"Everyday, before they undertake any work, they burn incense in the said mosques [temples] and sometimes they sacrifice their own persons... they take many boys or girls, and even grown men and women, and in the presence of those idols they open their breasts, while they are alive, and take out the hearts and entrails, and burn the said entrails and hearts before the idols, offering that smoke in sacrifice to them."

That's as much detail I will give about their methods of sacrifice. I bring this up only because the Spanish were terrified of this happening to them. To prevent a possible mutiny, Cortez became pretty tyrannical. When he heard of a possible mutiny, he hung some of the ringleaders, lashed others and even had his fleet of ships burned down to prevent anybody from returning to Cuba, stranding him and his men on the mainland.

The Spaniards are soon greeted by the Aztec representatives bearing gifts. When they arrived, they adorned Cortez with regalia. I guess not trusting the intentions of the Aztecs, Cortez replied by saying "Is this all?", seized the men and decided to introduce them to their cannons. From the Florentine Codex:

"Then the Captain ordered that they be tied up; they put irons on their feet and necks. When this was done, they fired the large cannon. One by one they fainted, they fell to the deck; swaying, they lost consciousness. And the Spaniards lifted and raised them and gave them some wine to drink. Then they gave them food, fed them. With this, they recovered their strength and caught their breath."

Cortez then challenged the messengers to a fight, but this was too much for the mere messengers who begged to be released. When they were, the representatives returned to Tenochtitlan and relayed back to Moctezuma what they had seen.

The Spanish, learning of Moctezuma, decided to take four hundred of their men with fifteen horses and march towards Tenochtitlan, leaving two hundred in Veracruz. Of Their first stop was to a settlement called Cempoala, who gave them a cheerful reception, but while they were there, five Aztec tax collectors arrived and asked the tribe for tribute. Cortez decided to take the tax collectors prisoner, but later released them,

Totonac. As allies, the Totonac would help the Spanish build Veracruz.

When Moctezuma's greeters returned. He asked them to meet him at a temple and had some captives sacrificed. After the sacrifices, he spread their blood on the chest of the messengers before allowing them to tell him what they had seen. They told winning the favor of the Cempoala people, who were called the Moctezuma of the Spaniards, their food, and their superiority.

"He was even more frightened when he heard how the cannon exploded on command, sounding like thunder... And when it was fired, something like a ball of stone comes out... shooting sparks and raining fire... and punishes the head even to the brain and causes discomfort... when it struck a tree, it splintered, seeming to vanish, as if someone blew it away... When Moctezuma heard all this, he was filled with terror, as if he were fainting. His heart was sickened; his heart was anguished."

The Aztec King decided to now send a whole slew of magicians, ambassadors and warriors to Cortez with gifts and supplies of food, sacrifices, gold and cloth as a thank you for releasing his tax collectors. He also praised Cortez with adulation, making his belief known that he thought the Spaniards were gods, but also tried to dissuade Cortez from visiting the city. Of course though, once Cortez knew Tenochtitlan had gold, there was no stopping him from coming.

Moctezuma, now probably convinced that Cortes was

Quetzalcoatl, figured that as gods, he and his men probably liked sacrificial blood on their food. The Spaniards were disgusted when they were presented with bloody meals and new meals were later prepared. That night, Moctezuma's magicians tried to cast spells on the Spanish, hoping they would soon leave, but nothing worked. They returned to the Capitol and told their King, "We are no match for them". They also told Moctezuma that the Spanish had a Mayan women with them and had been asking lots of questions about him. Frightened, he pondered about what to do next. Should he leave, fight, or stay? In the end, he decided to stay and wait it out.

The Spanish marched until he arrived near the city of Tlaxcala, whose people are enemies of the Aztecs. The Tlaxcalans weren't happy to see the Spaniards so they attacked them at first. Violence, violence and more violence commenced: Early in September 1519, the Tlaxcalans fought three different battles with Cortez and his men before realizing that the Spaniards could be of use to them in their war with the Aztecs. They then took the Spaniards to their city and after exchanging gifts and having a little chat about Jesus, they made an alliance.

Staying with the Aztec enemy for so long may or may not have prompted Moctezuma to order a trap for the Spaniards. His ambassadors urged Cortez to march to Tenochtitlan through a route that led them through a city called Cholula. Cholula was home of the largest pyramid in the Americas. It's so large that, though the great Egyptian Pyramid in Giza is taller, Cholula's pyramid has a larger footprint.

With the Totonac and Tlaxcala joining his forces, Cortez and his men began marching west until they made it to Cholula. The Tlaxcalans were asked to stay back as Cortez and his men entered the city. Either out of paranoia or keen judgement that the Cholulans were going to kill and eat them, they gathered all the nobles, priests, and such, asking to meet them at a local courtyard. Believing the Cholulans were going to kill him and his men in their sleep, Cortez cried out "Royal laws command that treason cannot remain unpunished; for your crime, you must die!" They then shot the men in the courtyard, then brought in the Tlaxcalans to slaughter the rest of the town, killing an estimated three thousand people in three hours, and even went as far as to burn some Cholulans alive. They then burned the city to the ground.

After this, with little choice left, Moctezuma invited Cortez and his men to Tenochtitlan. There were two roads that led there from Cholula and Moctezuma's men advised them to take one of the routes. Cortez took the other. Moctezuma sent out wizards and priests, but they couldn't even meet up with Cortes, much less cast a spell on him. Even if they did, spells wouldn't work, greed was much more powerful. They returned to tell Moctezuma the news. When he heard it, he was saddened and said:

"What can we do, my strong ones? What can be done here? We are finished! We are at the mercy of our gods! Is there a mountain we can climb? Can we perhaps escape? We are at the mercy of our gods . . . What they want, they will get, what they

want will come to be."

They decided to prepare to greet Cortez and his men. Flowers and other decorations began to pop up around the city.

Meanwhile, the Spaniards and their native friends continued to Tenochtitlan. Passing between the mountains of Iztaccihuatl and Popocatepetl, they decided to investigate Popocatepetl, for it appeared to be a smokey volcano, but with a snow cap in a warm climate. They confirmed what they had seen, but couldn't figure out what caused it. While up there though, Cortez's men set their eyes on the city they had been looking for. It was set on a small island in the middle of a large lake, connected to the mainland by bridges, or causeways that can be lifted to allow canoes to pass, looking like a paradise getaway; the Spanish must have been astonished.

After setting eyes on the city, the Spaniards made it to one of the causeways that entered into the city of Tenochtitlan by November 8, 1519, and was greeted by about a thousand fully dressed inhabitants. As Cortez passed each one, they individually greeted him, which took up a lot of time. Once he made it past the causeway, he met Moctezuma. Cortez walked up to salute him, but was stopped by Moctezuma's men, who then performed the same greeting to him. The Aztec King walked up to Cortez and gave him some flowers and necklaces before giving a speech:

"Our lord, you are very welcome in your arrival in this land. You

have come to satisfy your curiosity about your noble city of Mexico. You have come here to sit on your throne, to sit under its canopy, which I have kept for awhile for you... I am not just dreaming that I have seen you and have looked at you face to face. I have been worried for a long time, looking toward the unknown from which you have come, the mysterious place. For our rulers departed, saying that you would come to your city and sit upon your throne. And now it has been fulfilled, you have returned. Go enjoy your palace, rest your body. Welcome our lords to this land."

They then walked hand in hand as friends to Moctezuma's palace where he presented Cortez with more gold and talked about the tale of Quetzalcoatl, submitting himself to Cortez. He also apparently flashed his naked body to Cortez during this encounter to prove that he was just a man and not a god, like he thought Cortez was. In the end, he said this to Cortez:

"It is true I have some things of gold..."

That being all he needed to know, Cortez probably stopped paying attention, but more was said...

"It is true I have some things of gold, which my ancestors have left me; all that I have is at your service whenever you wish it. I am now going to my other houses where I reside; you will be here provided with every thing necessary for yourself and your people, and will suffer no embarrassment, as you are in your own house and country."

For the next six days, Cortez and his men rested.

Cortez was amazed at the town he had set out to reach, especially their large temples. After walking all the way to the top of their main temple, Cortez decided that he wanted a cross erected, which caused the first bit of awkwardness between the two groups, since he wanted to mess around with their sacred places. The second bit of awkwardness came when Cortez received word that a group of Aztecs had killed seven Spaniards back in Veracruz. The killers were caught and had fingered Moctezuma before being burned to death. After that, Cortez lured Moctezuma, his family and many nobles back into the palace where he was seized and held prisoner. Residents tried to rebel, but the sound of a cannon changed their minds. The next day, the Spanish had the residents gather supplies; chickens, cooking pots, and water pitchers. Knowing that Moctezuma was still a popular leader, Cortez decided to keep him alive as a puppet ruler, which worked for six tense months.

1520 - 1521

Despite being held prisoner in his own kingdom, Moctezuma made friends with Cortez. He gave Cortez the fortune left to him by his father, which was estimated at about forty two thousand pounds of gold. Score! Cortez took the gold and had it all melted down into bars.

"And when they arrived, when they entered the house of treasures, it was like they had arrived in Paradise. They searched everywhere and coveted everything, for, yes, they were

dominated by their greed."

He had learned of the city's three main sources of gold, and had crosses erected at the main temple, which pissed off the Aztec people, who began to see the Spanish gods as the greedy men that they were. Whispers of rebellion began to spread in the city and Aztec priests began to receive messages from their gods, threatening to leave them if they did not drive the Spanish away. When the priests told Moctezuma, he warned Cortez.

In April of 1520 Cortez learned that eighteen ships, with fourteen thousand men, had come looking for him. He knew who they were: They were men sent from Cuba by Governor Velázquez. Instead of waiting for them to come to him though, Cortez decided to go to them. He took his most capable men and native warriors and began to march them east to confront Governor Velázquez's men, leaving a small guard of men in the hands of a handsome red-headed man named Pedro de Alvarado to watch over Moctezuma. That man will start some serious problems soon.

Pamphilo de Narvaez, ordered by Velasquez to find and return Cortez dead or alive, landed at Veracruz in April of 1520. His motto for this mission was "Viva quien vence!" which was Spanish for "Long live the victorious!" Some of the men Cortez left behind were grateful that somebody had come to their rescue. Narvaez wined and dined these men, who told them everything that had happened since the voyage began. He then led a group to the village of Cempoala, with the ambition of meeting Cortez in Tenochtitlan.

Narvaez had been outsmarted however: Believing that Cortez knew nothing of their arrival, and thinking he outnumber his party by a factor of three, Narvaez believed that he would have no problem catching the fugitive. Narvaez also didn't count on the fact that he himself wasn't a very good captain and as a result had a group of men put on rations for saying they would rather join Cortez. It's possible that Juan Rodriguez Cabrillo, the young captain who had gone with Narvaez, was part of this group. Cortez however, did know of Narvaez's arrival and by now had amassed an alliance of over a thousand native warriors in response. He took his army, marched toward Veracruz and ambushed Narvaez, which happened in Cempoala. From Cortez's second letter:

"On Easter day, a little after midnight, I marched for the quarters of Narvaez... When I reached the city Narvaez had all his men in full armor, and the horses caparisoned, in complete readiness, and two hundred men guarded every square... In one of these towers were Narvaez was quartered, the staircase was defended by nineteen matchlocks; but we mounted it with such rapidity that they had not time to put fire to more than one of the pieces, which, it pleased God, did not go off, nor occasion any injury. So our men ascended the tower until they reached the apartment of Narvaez, where he and about fifty of his men fought with alguazil mayor and the rest that had gone up, and although the latter called upon them many times to surrender to your Highness, they refused until the building was set on fire,

when they last gave in."

Narvaez was now wounded and had been taken prisoner. Defeated, most of these men switched sides. Cortez told Narvaez's men that he had found an island paradise full of gold and women, and if they would return there with him, he would regale them with riches. He had freed the men who were put on rations and ordered special treatment for them. More men switched, including what was possibly a now freed Juan Rodriguez Cabrillo. Now that that was over with, Cortez decided to stay at Cempoala for a bit of rest before returning to Tenochtitlan. He sent a messenger back to the city to relay the news.

There was one more notable passenger who came with Narvaez, he was Francisco Eguía, an African slave. Since Columbus' voyages, the native population in the Caribbean had become enslaved to the Spanish. They were forced to grow crops, mine gold, and build towns. Many natives died as a result of being overworked or underfed, and things got so bad that many natives chose to commit suicide. Needless to say, the native population shrank dramatically which led to a shortage of slaves. Meanwhile, Portugal had established settlements throughout the African coast and saw an opportunity to enslave the native population there. It appears there were so many African slaves that they started to export them... the beginnings of the slave trade.

Back in Cuba and Hispaniola, more and more native slaves

began to be replaced by African slaves, including Eguía. It is believed that Eguía however, didn't travel alone. Unbeknownst to himself or anyone else at the time, he carried a virus on him. It was a virus that he was immune to, but the native populations of these continents weren't: Smallpox.

Meanwhile, back in Tenochtitlan, Alvarado and the men left behind were invited to be guests at the Aztec's Tóxcatl festival. This festival had the usual dancing and sacrifices, but Alvarado couldn't take anymore sacrifices, either that or he became frightened and thought they were going to sacrifice him. From the Florentine codex:

"The procession began, and everyone went into the temple patio in order to dance "The Dance of the Snake."... If anyone showed disobedience or was not in his proper order, they struck him in the hips, on the legs, and on the shoulders. Then they violently tossed him out of the patio, beating him and shoving him to the ground, and they dragged him outside with his face in the dirt by the ears... At this time, when everyone was enjoying the fiesta, when everyone was already dancing, when everyone was already singing, when song was linked to song and the songs roared like waves, in that precise moment the Spaniards determined to kill people. They came to the patio, armed for battle."

Alvarado ordered his men to block the exits and had most of the people involved in the festival, including many nobles killed. This episode is notably violent in the Florentine codex as it described body parts being cut off.

"Some tried to escape, but the Spaniards murdered them at the gates while they laughed. Others climbed the walls, but they could not save themselves. Others lay down among the victims and pretended to be dead. But if they stood up again they (the Spaniards) would see them and kill them... Then a roar was heard, screams, people wailed, as they beat their palms against their lips. Quickly the captains assembled, as if planned in advance, and carried their spears and shields. Then the battle began. (The Aztecs) attacked them with arrows and even javelins, used for hunting birds. They furiously hurled their javelins (at the Spaniards)."

This event turned the tide of favor against the Spanish and whatever the Aztecs once liked about them were now eclipsed by this massacre. City residents began to indiscriminately attack the Spanish who then retreated back to Moctezuma's palace, becoming trapped inside. Twelve days after Cortez sent his messenger to Tenochtitlan, the messenger had returned to Cempoala with a batch of letters for Cortez. From his letters to the King:

"(t)he Indians had attacked the garrison on all sides, and set fire to it in many places; that they had sunk mines about it, placing our people in imminent danger; all of whom would perish, unless Moctezuma should command the hostile operations to cease... It was added, that a great part of their supplies had been forcibly seized, and that the enemy had burned the four

brigantines (ships) I had built there; and finally, that our people were in extreme distress, and begged me to come to their aid with the greatest possible haste."

With that, Cortez and his men packed up and returned to Tenochtitlan.

He returned on June 24, 1520 to an eerily quiet city and headed right for the palace. Cortez' men rejoiced in his return and for the next couple of days, all was well and quiet. With everything seemingly fine, Cortez decided to send a message back to Veracruz. Half an hour later however, the messenger returned battered, bruised and freaking out. The natives had raised the draw bridges, blocked streets, beat him to a pulp and were heading in mass towards the palace with arms. Soon, rocks and arrows began to rain over the walls of the fortress to the roars of angry jeers, wounding many Spaniards including Cortez himself. Fires were lit, so the Spanish cut the flaming portion of the fortress wall away and knocked it down, extinguishing some of it, before posting guards to keep the natives from breaching the grounds.

According to Cortes' letters, they fought into the night, and over eighty Spaniards were wounded that day. That night, they attempted to have the breached walls repaired. The following day, the Aztecs returned and resumed the battle. Even with thirteen long guns, called "arquebusses", and skilled crossbow men like Cabrillo, the Spanish were almost overwhelmed by the number of forces that came to attack. About fifty to sixty

Spaniards were wounded as a result.

The Spanish forces who weren't fighting it out were ordered to construct three "engines of timber" to block all the arrows and rocks being hurled at them, they also gathered all the iron weapons they could. Moctezuma, still loyal to Cortez, asked to speak to his people to try and calm them down. He went out onto the balcony of the palace, in front of the crowd of angry Aztecs and tried to sue for peace. In response, a rock from the crowd was thrown at Moctezuma and hit him in the head. From Cortes' Letters:

"I caused him (Moctezuma) to be taken up, and when he reached a battlement projecting from the fortress, and sought an opportunity to address the people who were fighting in that quarter, a stone thrown by some one of his own subjects struck him on the head with so much force that he died three days later. I then gave his dead body to two indians who were amongst the prisoners and taking it upon their shoulders, they bore it away to his people; what afterwards became of it I know not."

Some say that Cortez forced him to speak to his people and when he learned that the King was no longer favored, Cortez killed him, though we may never know. The Florentine Codex tells what happened to Moctezuma's body though:

"The Spaniards tossed the bodies of Moctezuma and Itzquauhtzin, who had died, on a place near the waters edge called Teoayoc... they hurried to take Moctezuma up in their

arms and brought him to a place called Copulco. There they placed him on a wooden pyre and set fire to it... and while the body of Moctezuma burned, some people, angry and without good will, chided him... And many others cursed him, screamed, lamented, and shook their heads."

So with the mighty King Moctezuma gone, a new man was chosen to lead the Aztecs, his name was Cuitlahuac. Besides the "engines of timber" which blocked projectiles, Cortez also had his men build a portable bridge made of timber to lay across the gaps of the causeways. Well... if by "portable", you buy the fact that it had to be carried by forty men. At this point, many of Cortez men had been wounded from previous fighting. He realized that he and his men had to escape in order to survive. They made their attempt on June 30, 1520. Before they left, Cortez allowed his men to raid Moctezuma's treasures. The greedy men they were, they grabbed as much as they could carry and snuck out of the palace that drizzling night:

"I took all the gold and jewels belonging to your majesty... and placed them in one apartment... and I begged and desired the alcaldes, regidores, and all the people to aid me in removing and perserving this treasure; I gave up my mare to carry as much as she could bear; and I selected certain Spaniards, as well as my own servants as others, to accompany the gold and the mare..."

Besides treasure, Cortez took Moctezuma's son and two of his daughters with him. Cortes led an advance guard that was commanded by Alverado. Alverado was in charge of the a hundred and fifty Spanish and four hundred Tlaxcalins as well as the "portable" bridge.

They reached the causeway with the least amount of guards, were able to fight them off, carried the bridge over the first gap and walked across. However, either the guards, or a women fetching water and witnessed the event made such a racket, that it wasn't long before numerous Aztec warriors assembled. They came from the street and from the water in numerous canoes, fully armed. Before the Spaniards could get the bridge over to the second gap, they had become fully engaged in fighting and had to abandon it. Cortez, some horsemen and a hundred others including Juan Rodriguez Cabrillo, were able to swim across the other gaps to relative safety, but many of his men weren't so lucky.

The warriors and Spaniards still on the causeways were being pelted with arrows and pushed off. Many who tried to swim across were weighed down by the amount of treasure they tried to carry and drowned. They shot back with guns, but were overwhelmed by the number of forces. The bodies soon piled so high in the shallow waters that Pedro de Alvarado, who had ordered the massacre that started this whole mess, was able to barely escape by running across the causeway gap over piles of bodies. From the Florentine codex:

"And when the Spaniards arrived... it was as thought they had fallen off a precipice. They all fell... Soon the canal was

*completely full of them, full to the banks. But those who came at
the rear just passed and crossed over on people, on bodies."*
From Cortez's letters:

*"Leaving the people who formed this advanced party, I returned
to the rear, where I found troops hotly engaged; it is incalculable
how much our people suffered... besides the loss of all the gold,
jewels, cotton cloth, and many other things we had brought
away including the artillery."*

They had lost much of their men, gold, supplies, and weapons.
Even worse, they had lost the city they were once welcomed to.
Realizing how much he had lost in his retreat, Cortez leaned
against a tree and wept. This night is known to the Spanish as
"La Noche Triste" or "The Sad Night".

Their retreat didn't end there however. For the next two weeks,
the Spaniards continued to fall back, with the Aztecs constantly
on their trail, even after leaving Aztec lands. They soon arrived
at the Tlaxcalan city of Gualipan, where they were able to rest
for a few days. Unfortunately, they had to pay for all of their
provisions with what little gold they had left. They left after
three days for another city but three days later, fought another
battle with the Aztecs on July 14th, with more heavy losses
including Montezuma's son and daughters. They had originally
come to Tenochtitlan with four hundred men from Cortez's
voyage. Out of an incredible amount of charm and charisma, he
was able to add about another fifteen hundred to two thousand
more men in the form of Spaniards from Narvaez's voyage and

native allies Cortez picked up along the way. By the time they finally made it back to Tlaxcala territory however, they had only four hundred and fourty people left, all of which were wounded. The Tlaxcalans gave the survivors sanctuary in their land.

Back in Tenochtitlan, probably believing that they had rid themselves of the Spanish for good, the Aztecs began to rebuild their city, but soon, awful things began to happen to their bodies. First they became sick with flu like symptoms, then their bodies began developing red spots that would completely envelop them. Many died in terrible agony. The outbreak wasn't just isolated to Tenochtitlan however, the same disease was also affecting the Tlaxcalans.

Since Narvaez's landing, smallpox had begun to spread from village to village. First to Tepeaca, then to Tlaxcala. Noticing that the Spaniards did not pick up the virus, many Tlaxcalans asked to be baptized, believing that their Christian god prevented the Spaniards from being infected. The outbreak passed in Tlaxcala and with Cortez somewhat recovered from his wounds, he decided to return to Tenochtitlan in force.

Looking back at his escape, Cortes realized that, had the Aztecs destroyed the the causeways leading out of the city, he and his men would have been trapped there. With this in mind, his new plan was to take control of Lake Texcoco, which held the city, and to starve out the residents. Also, he needed to build ships, lots of ships.

Over a period of months, he prepared. Friendly ships from Cuba and Spain were soon docking in port, so Cortes sent what was left of Narvaez' expedition back to Spain... except for Cabrillo. He stayed behind and led a group of Tlaxcalans in building Cortes' new fleet of brigantines. Thirteen ships were built in pieces that would be transported to the lake and put together. Next, Cabrillo and his team went into the forest to find materials needed to caulk the ships once they were built. Caulking is basically a way to waterproof ships by making a special tar and applying it to the hull. They couldn't find the beef tallow needed to make the tar though, so Cabrillo decided to use the gruesome alternative of human tallow from the dead.

Being tactical now, Cortes also sent advanced parties to Tenochtitlan to survey the lake in anticipation for the siege.

The Tlaxcalans then carried the ship pieces to another place called Tezuco and began assembling and caulking them. From there, a canal was dug to Lake Texcoco which took fifty days and about eight-thousand people to accomplish. Once they were built, the ships were blessed and boarded. By April 28, 1521, Cortes was given over ten thousand Tlaxcalan warriors by their leader, who was now baptized as a Christian.

Back in the ancient city, the deaths were getting worse:

"(People) with the illness could not walk, they could only lay in their dwellings and sleeping places. They could not move; they could not stir; they could not change position, nor lie on one

side, nor face down, nor on their backs. And when they sturred, they screamed. The pustules that covered people caused great desolation; a great many people died of them, and many just died of hunger; no one took care of others any longer."

That same December, Cuitlahuac, the man chosen to lead the Aztecs after Moctezuma, had also died of Smallpox. The man chosen next to lead was named Cuahtémoc.

April 1521. After seventy days of death, the city of Tenochtitlan was devastated. Their leader, Moctezuma, was dead; and disease had run rampant through the city, killing the next Aztec ruler, Cuitlahuac. Cuahtémoc, Moctezuma's cousin, was the ruler of whatever was left.

Meanwhile, Cortes and his men, who had barely escaped Tenochtitlan with their lives, were ready to make a comeback. When all was set, he sent a division of men led by Alvarado to a city called Cuyoacan and another division to Tacuba. He sent a third division of men to Iztapalapa, a nearby city next to the lake, to attack it. He then boarded one of the brigantines and set sail towards Iztapalapa. Natives of that city spotted the ships as they neared from their high temples and immediately began making smoke signals to warn everyone around the lake. Cortes and his men went on shore along a steep hill, taking over trenches and killing everyone they saw except women and children.

A mass of over five-hundred canoes then began to enter the lake.

Cortes saw this and immediately boarded his ship, but ordered this crew to wait for the canoes to come to them. Before they got too close though, the canoes stopped. I'm picturing a tense stand off moment where the two sides stare each other down. Then Cortes felt the direction of the wind change. The change was to his advantage, so he ordered his men to break through the lines and to chase down the canoes. His letters describe what happened next:

"As the wind was fair, we bore down upon the midst of them, and although they fled as fast as possible, we broke an immense number of canoes, and destroyed many of the enemy in a style worthy of admiration. In the chase we followed them full three long leagues, till they were locked up amongst the houses of the city; and thus it pleased our Lord to grant us a greater and more complete victory than we had ventured to ask or desire."

Upon seeing the ships crush the canoes, some of Alvarado's division soon began to march to Tenochtitlan to enter the city but were fought back. Night fell, so as they rested, Cortes and Alvarado made plans to siege the city again in the morning. This time, they would use the cannons.

The next day, Cortes and his men marched to Tenochtitlan with the intention of taking the city back. They fought through more trenches guarded by men before they made it to the causeway, fighting through with the help of the brigantines, and eventually to the city entrance. From the Florentine Codex:

"and when they had prepared the canons, they fired at the wall. The wall cracked and broke open. And the Second time it was hit, the wall fell to the ground, destroyed... the great warriors in vain took refuge behind the stone columns... None of them would come out into the open."

Then the men from the ships started to disembark for the siege.

As cannon smoke fulled the air, blocking the Spaniard's view, many Aztec warriors fled into the city to get more help. Help came, and the two forces clashed. Stones and arrows flew, swords swung, and horses charged. When the Aztecs came in their canoes, they now had to contend with the ships that were now on the attack. It got too intense though and both sides retreated. Cortes claims he could have entered the city, but there were too many Aztecs on buildings and roofs who kept lobbing arrows and rocks at them. Since they had the advantage of height, Cortes decided at this point that if he's going to take the city, he was going to have to burn those buildings to the ground.

Over the next few weeks there were more skirmishes in the streets of the city. The Spanish would spend the day taking the trenches and causeways and burning the city, then retreat back to camp for the night, while the ships patrolled the waters. The Aztecs would then take back the city, causeway and trenches at night and the next morning, the Spanish would return and everyone would do it again. Patrolling the waters of Lake Texcoco prevented the dying Aztecs from leaving the island to get help or supplies. They were now dying of disease and hunger and becoming more desperate.Alverado took a different strategy. He set up sentries (guards) to keep the causeways and bridges under his control at night. He made it into the market place, but before he could get his horsemen in, the Aztecs overwhelmed them and forced them to retreat. Still, he took so much territory that Cortes arrived and was impressed by how far he had gotten. While inspecting the causeways, a group of Aztecs attacked them. In this attack, Cortes seemed to have a moment of shell shock as he described the deaths of some of the men who tried to protect him as he tried to save a few of his men from drowning. Here is an extensive excerpt from his letters:

"As this affair was so sudden and I saw them killing our men, I resolved to remain there, and perish in the fight... Several Indians of the enemy already advanced to seize me, and would have borne me off had it not been for a captain of fifty men whom I always had with me and a youth in his company, to whom God I owed my life; and in saving mine, like a valiant man, he lost his own... The captain who was with me, Antonio de Quinones, said to me, "Let us leave, this place and save your life..."...we began to retreat... at this moment there came up a servant of mine on horseback, and made a little room; but presently he received a blow in his threat from a lance thrown from a low terrace that brought him to the ground... I mounted the horse, but not to fight... two mares on which two of my servants rode fell on the causeway into the water; one of them was killed by the Indians, but the other was saved by some of the infantry. Another servant of mine, Cristobal de Guzman, rode a horse they gave him at the little island to bring to me, on which

I might make my escape; but the enemy killed both him and the horse before he reached me... some of the enemy threw in the way two or three heads of Christian men from the upper part of an entrenchment where they were fighting..."

In the retreat, they left one of their cannons and some Aztecs captured it and dragged it into the water. The Spanish also lost their "standard" in the retreat, which is basically the flag they carried into battle. The Aztecs had also captured some Spaniards, horses and Tlaxcalans and dragged them back to their temple, where they were sacrificed one by one. They then cut the heads off of the Spaniards and their horses, putting the heads on stakes. That night, the Aztecs celebrated. The message was clear: Tenochtitlan would not fall willingly.

As a way to intimidate the Spaniards, the Aztecs sent messengers with horse heads telling the Spanish that their heads would be next. This didn't stop them from besieging the city daily, except now, Cortes decided that as he took the city block by block, he would burn the buildings on both sides to prevent anybody from attacking them from above. In this way, he took the market back.

At one point, the Aztecs called out for peace. Cortes asked the men to bring their sovereign to make it official, then waited for him to come. In reality, there was no intention of peace. The Aztecs had scattered rocks all over the square and began hurling them at the Spaniards, so the Spanish charged the square, but the rocks made it hard for the horses to navigate. This didn't stop the Christians from advancing and burning more buildings. The next day, they got so far, that they made it to the square of their grand temple and Cortez ascended to the top:

"I ascended the highest tower that the Indians might know me, as I was sensible that it would disturb them much to see me in that place."

From the tower, Cortes was able to see the whole city and determined that he had destroyed about 7/8ths of it. Understanding that it was only a matter of time before the last eighth was taken, Cortes decided to sue for peace. However, at this point, nothing was going to stop what remained of the Aztecs from fighting to the death. Later, the Spanish got creative and set up a catapult to throw rocks over the remaining walls, but they couldn't get the aim right and ended up fighting each other over the contraption.

After three months, with many of their people dead from either war, disease, or starvation, the Aztecs were feeling pretty helpless. Then this happened:

"When night had fallen, it rained and sprinkled off and on Then in the deepest darkness of the night there appeared in the heavens what was like a fire. It looked and appeared as if it was coming from the sky, like a whirlwind; it went spinning around and revolving. The blazing, turning ember seemed to explode; it was as if embers burst out of it--some very large, some very small, some like sparks. It rose up like a coppery wind; it arose,

crackling, snapping, and exploding loudly. Then it circled the walls at the water, heading toward Coyonacazco, then it went into the midst of the lake and disappeared there No one struck his hand against his mouth; no one uttered a word."

This seemed to have startled both sides, for there was no fighting the next morning, August 13, 1521. Instead, there was a meeting of Aztec nobles, including Cuahtémoc. They took the event the previous night as an omen and discussed what they should do next. Cortes had asked to see Cuahtémoc, but Cuahtémoc preferred to die than to deal with Cortes. However, this time Cuahtémoc decided that it was time for him to surrender, so he got on a boat with a couple of servants and was rowed out towards the Spanish.

A brigantine spotted a canoe and prepared to attack it until the people inside signaled who was in the canoe. When they made it to land, Cuahtémoc was captured and brought to Cortes. Cortes asked Cuahtémoc to sit, but Cuahtémoc refused and asked Cortes to strike him dead with a dagger. Cortes had no need to kill Cuahtémoc... yet. The important thing was that he had him, and he knew where all that gold went.

They then proceeded to bombard the city with more canon fire. Finally, the population had had enough and began to flee. Since the causeways were blocked, people either took canoes or waded in the waters of Lake Texcoco, some neck deep. Some had to carry their children over their heads. The Spanish and their native allies then went on a rampage, robbing fleeing residents of their gold and women. To avoid being captured and raped, women covered themselves in mud, but it was no use. The leadership of Tenochtitlan was gone, its buildings and temples destroyed, and its people either dead or deserted. The city was now in the hands of Cortes and his men. The battle of Tenochtitlan was over.

Somehow, out of crazy luck and legendary smooth talk, Cortes had beaten some incredible odds. His first act was to ban human sacrifice and replaced all of the Aztec idols with crosses and such. He let Cuahtémoc live until 1525. The surviving Aztecs were moved to a nearby town, while the city was cleaned up. In time, the ashes would blow away, the blood wiped clean and in the footprint of Tenochtitlan, a new city would rise named in honor of the Aztecs, otherwise known as the Mexicas.

Tenochtitlan would now forever be known as "Mexico City".

Seven - Juan Rodriguez Cabrillo
Tying Up Loose Ends...

During the Conquest of Mexico, Ferdinand Magellan was on his own Spanish expedition to open up the spice trade. In 1519, he left Europe with five ships and by December, made his way to Rio de Janeiro. Magellan and his crew continued to sail after spending Christmas there, arriving at St. Julian where three of his ships mutinied. Angered at the attempt, he had one of the leaders of the mutiny beheaded. He then entered the conveniently named Straits of Magellan, ordering his men to fire their guns when they reached the other side.

It took 36 days to sail through the strait, but once he crossed into the South Sea, Magellan noticed how much calmer it was than the stormy seas he had just left, and he renamed the South Sea "Mar Pacifico", or the Peaceful Sea. By March of 1521, he reached Guam where the natives stole one of his skiffs. In retaliation for the theft, he went inland until he found a native village and burned it down before setting sail for the Philippines. While there, Magellan was taken to the city of Cebu where he baptized the royal family and eight hundred others, burning villages that refused to convert, so between him and Cortez, the pattern of cultures killing other cultures continued. Eventually one village of natives overwhelmed him and he died at Mactan in 1521. Not a lot of people survived these voyages, the expedition returned in 1522 with only nineteen people.

After the fall of Tenochtitlan, Cortes was granted governorship of the newly dubbed Mexico City, but he wasn't trusted enough to become its Viceroy, instead, the title of Viceroy was given to one of Cortes' rivals, Antonio de Mendoza. By 1525, Cortes had executed Cuahtémoc, the last Aztec King, and was fighting in the region of Honduras to expand his control. Cortez and his translator, Malintzin begin having babies and his deeds were honored by the King of Spain, who gave him his own Coat of Arms. Alverado founded the city of Santiago before helping Cortes conquer more lands, and right alongside them was Juan Rodriguez Cabrillo. Cabrillo was given a large plot of good grazing land and ownership of any natives living there, receiving his title in January 1529. He had natives pay him tribute in the form of grown foods and had them working in gold mines, making him a rich man. Cabrillo owned slaves.

Meanwhile in Spain, the Spanish King Charles the First was profiting greatly from all of the expeditions and conquests. They helped to solidify his rule, and convinced him of his mission to spread Christianity throughout the world. He also had an interesting idea: For some time, explorers had searched for a water passage through the American Continent in order to reach Asia, where a real profit could be made. But over twenty years' worth of voyages had failed to find one. Charles had an interesting solution: If they couldn't find a water passage through the Americas, perhaps they could try to build one: The plan was to construct a canal through the Isthmus of Panama. However, it was never started during the King's life time.

In 1533, Cortez paid for a one ship expedition, in charge of searching for a previous expedition that was looking for a northwest passage through the Americas led by Diego de Becerra. But Becerra was killed in a revolt led by one of his crewman, Fortún Ximénez. They then landed in what they thought was an offshore island, but in reality, it was on the enormous Baja California peninsula. Ximénez himself, was soon killed by the natives of this "island" and the survivors of the voyage returned to Mexico City. Cortez, being told of the island, decided to check it out.

Meanwhile, in 1534, Cabrillo took his ship, the San Salvador, on a voyage of trade. The trip helped pay for the construction of the new ship and trained the crew for future voyages. In 1535, Cortez set out on a voyage, arriving at present day La Paz and establishing a temporary colony there that he called Santa Cruz. In 1539 Cortez paid for a three ship expedition up the Pacific Coast, hiring Francisco de Ulloa to lead it. Ulloa found the "island" coast on July 8th and named the waters between the lands, or the present day Gulf of California, the "Sea of Cortez". Ulloa went up the west coast of the continent, and tried to sail up the peninsula but had to turn back due to strong winds. Once he returned however he was stabbed to death. Ulloa wasn't well recognized for this feat at the time, because though he explored the peninsula as what it was... a peninsula and not an island, cartographers were still creating maps of the Americas depicting the Baja Peninsula of California as an island.

After a Spanish priest boasted of seeing a golden city in North America, a land expedition of almost four thousand men set out February 23, 1540 from Compostela, Mexico headed by

Francisco Vasquez de Coronado. Sailing the Sea of Cortez, they then rowed up the Colorado River, hoping that it led to a passage to the Atlantic, and also in search for the mythical city of gold. When they needed supplies, they would head to the nearest native village and demand supplies, which sometimes led to skirmishes between them and the natives. In turn, word of these skirmishes would travel all around the region through native trade routes until eventually reaching the Ipai and Tipai. To cover more ground, Coronado split his expedition in two; one to follow the Colorado River, and one to follow a native guide named "The Turk" who had bragged about seeing this city himself and had promised to show Coronado the way.

Hearing of all these things, Viceroy Mendoza sent Hernando de Alarcón to verify the discoveries. He set out in 1540, completing Ulloa's voyage, and entering the Colorado river. In describing the land, Alarcón sarcastically referred to it as "California", referring to the mythical island in the famous book. Apparently the name stuck.

Meanwhile, Cabrillo was well off: Married with children and rich, but with more money came more problems. His land soon became the subject of disputes and eventually, lawsuits. He soon needed money, luckily he had connections. Alverado had decided to return to Spain to take care of some business and so commissioned Cabrillo to build a fleet of ships while he was away. After picking the place and getting the Viceroy's blessing, Cabrillo then focused his attention on building the small fleet of ships.

While Cabrillo was busy building ships, Coronado's team had failed in their expedition. When Coronado finally reached his destination and looked upon what he thought would be a city of gold, he instead saw large clusters of native adobe homes. Boy was he pissed! Wouldn't you be? Before returning back to Mexico City, he had the Spanish priest sent home in disgrace, and had The Turk strangled. Coronado never found the golden city and returned to Mexico City in March of 1542 empty handed and facing possible war crimes. However, he did make it all the way up to modern day Kansas and the other part of his expedition "discovered" what would later be known as the Grand Canyon.

Back in Spain, Charles the First was traveling by carriage, when a man forced his way through a crowd of onlookers, demanding an audience with the King. Irritated by the nerve of the man, the King came out and demanded to know who this person was and what he wanted. He probably asked something like "Who do you think you are to demand my time?" to which the man may have replied, "I am a man who has given you more provinces than your ancestors left you cities". The man demanding the King's attention was Hernan Cortez, and he had indeed left him more provinces than his ancestors did. Over the years however, lawsuits and claims had been piling up for Cortez and so he decided to return to Spain to defend himself, but nobody would listen to him. His last bet was to appeal directly to the King. Feeling sorry for Cortez, the King allowed him to join one last voyage headed by Andrea Doria to the Barbary Coast. Cortez would be dead by 1547, famous but very bitter.

Between 1536 and 1540, Juan Rodriguez Cabrillo built seven or eight ships for Alvarado. After returning from a trip to Spain, Alvarado wrote to the King in 1539 saying that he had prepared an "armada to go on a voyage of discovery*". He had planned to split his fleet of ships into two groups to explore both the Pacific, and the Northern coast California.

Joining this fleet was the San Salvador, it was poised to be the flag ship of the coastal expedition. However, a sudden native revolt had forced Alvarado to run to the aid of the colonists. During the fight, a falling horse crushed him. He lived a few more days before dying, possibly in considerable pain.

Alvarado had tried to pay Cabrillo for his work by giving him land, but others were now challenging ownership of that land. Cabrillo himself had partially paid for the construction of the fleet on Alvarado's word that he would cover him, but now he was dead. Knowing he would have to appeal directly to the Spanish Crown for his payment, Cabrillo collected some statements to cover his ass and set sail for Guatemala for further instructions.

Cabrillo's Voyage

The Viceroy still wanted the trip to continue however, so by September 1541, Cabrillo made his way to a port town called Navidad, Mexico and finished preparing for his voyage. In June 27, 1542, a small fleet of two or three ships set sail from

Navidad. The fleet was to sail up the Pacific Coast to continue Ulloa's expedition up the west coast of the enormous "island" that lay beyond the Sea or Cortes. The main flagship was the two hundred ton galleon, San Salvador. The other ship was a one hundred ton galleon named the "Victoria".

If you've seen a galleon, it makes you wonder how it or the people inside were able to survive at sea. They're small, wooden vessels with multiple decks and masts. More sail than anything, and they don't look very easy to control. It wouldn't be fair to compare them to any of the ships that are active today (Well, except for the full size replica sitting in San Diego bay). I guess you can think of it as a slightly larger fishing boat made of wood and sails. As William E. Smythe put it:

"Quaint craft they were, with their round bows and square sterns and their poop decks rising in the air, so that they seemed about as high as they were long."

The first five days of Cabrillo's Expedition were uneventful, but on the 2nd of July, they had Baja California in view. Because of the bad weather though, it took them four days to cross over, anchoring at Punta de San Lucas. By the eleventh day, July 8th, they landed in an area called Punta Trinidad and waited for a storm to pass. They left Punta Trinidad on the 12th; passed Puerto San Pedro, and landed at a newly discovered port they called Madalena by the 19th. On July 20th they left Puerto Madalena. Stopping for food, water or firewood, they anchored at Punta Santa Catalina, Puerto Santiago, Punta Santa Ana, and

Puerto Fondo.

Beginning in August, they left for the next port, San Pedro
Vincula. Then they would anchor at the Islas San Estevan, Islas
Zedros, and Puerto Santa Clara. They noted that since reaching
the California coast, they had seen no natives on the shore. The
first time they saw any was a small group of four on the shore of
Puerto Santa Clara, who quickly fled. Because of bad winds,
they stayed there until August 13th. Two days later, they
anchored at Punta del Mal Abrigo. By the 20th, they had left San
Bernardo and landed at Punta Engano. On the 22nd, Cabrillo
went to shore and claimed the territory for Spain, renaming the
place Puerto La Posesion. They stayed for repairs until the 27th.
On the 31st, they found group of native fisherman, three of
which they hosted on the ship, but couldn't understand anything
they said by "signs" or improvised sign language, so they let
them go. They did have luck with another group of indians
though, who signed to them, saying there were other Spaniards
about five days inland, possibly the remains of the failed
Coronado Expedition. Cabrillo let the natives go with a letter to
carry to the Spaniards if they ran into them.

In the month of September, they continued up the coast,
anchoring on Islas San Agustin, Cabo de San Martin, and Cabo
de Cruz before landing in Puerto San Mateo on the 17th. They
left San Mateo on the 23rd of September and traveled along the
coast some 18 leagues. They then passed by three uninhabited
islands. He named them "Islas Desiertas", Spanish for "desert
islands". Beyond those islands, however, they saw clouds of

black smoke coming from the mainland: People were living here.

San Miguel

September 28, 1542, fifty years after Columbus made his historic voyage, Cabrillo and his fleet traveled about 6 more leagues before finding what they recorded as "a port, closed and very good". They wrote down the coordinates as 34 and 1/3 degrees and decided to set anchor at the mouth of the port, that was naturally covered in cobblestones between a raised hill, or as the Spanish call it "loma", and a couple of low lying sandbars.

In the Spaniard's attempt to please their god, much of the Spaniard's discoveries were named after saints and biblical references. Saints have their own day of celebration, where great feasts are held. For instance, the feast of Saint Michael fell on the following day, September 29th. The Spanish referred to Saint Michael as "San Miguel". So when Cabrillo and his fleet set anchor in this stable, natural harbor which they had never seen before, it seemed only appropriate for him to name the port "San Miguel". This is where traditional stories of this territory usually begin, with credit given to Cabrillo for "discovering" San Diego.

The Spaniards grabbed some articles to barter with and gifts to give, roped their sails, and prepared to go to shore. Because the bay seemed too shallow for the ships to travel through, a small group led by Cabrillo lowered a small boat and rowed toward the marshy shore. They soon began to see people on the shore.

They noticed that the people had gathered to watch them, but those people soon began to run away as the Spanish rowed closer to shore, leaving only three natives on the suddenly lonely and quiet beach to greet them. They continued to row towards the shore anyways, and upon landing, claimed the land for Spain with their usual flags and chanting. Then, they stood to greet the three remaining natives, who seemed very frightened.

Cabrillo and his men wore colorful uniforms, armored with polished metal breastplates, helmets, swords and crossbows. They're backed by a country that had conquered most of a continent. The three natives wore animal skins and painted faces. The rest of the natives, many of them simply butt-naked and frightened by the Spanish, had fled the area and were watching from a distance. Even if they did stand up to fight, their bows and arrows were no match for the Spanish powder and lead. They probably anticipated a slaughter of their people.

The pattern these writings follow would predict such a slaughter. Patterns however are not written in stone, they're just guides: Since Cabrillo was actually there on a voyage of discovery, our pattern breaks with him.

Instead of a slaughter, Cabrillo and his men gave the three native people presents. The journal doesn't say what they gave them; I'm assuming shirts. This may have surprised them all since they may have heard terrible stories from other villages of Guacamels, or white Christians, coming to kill and raid them to the south. Since neither group spoke the other's language, the natives used their best sign language to relate to Cabrillo that men looking like he and his men had passed through south-east of the mountains. The Ipai and Tipai wanted Cabrillo to know that they were afraid.

Overall, first contact was peaceful, so Cabrillo sent a few of his men up the river valley in search of fresh water, and a few other men to gather fish. Day gave way to night, and the group sent to gather fish returned to the San Salvador with three of their men wounded by arrows... opps. This was the first recorded instance of hostility in the region, luckily there was no retaliation. By the next morning, the men who were sent to find fresh water still hadn't returned and their shipmates were getting worried that they too had been attacked.

That wasn't the case however, they were simply lost. By the time the group had found water, it was nighttime. They retraced their steps back to the port by following the "drying out river" valley back, but literally took a wrong turn. When they reached what they thought was the same bay they had come from and didn't see the ships in the dark of night, they set up camp and spent the night there. There is no telling what must have gone through their heads at the time. They might have thought that the small fleet had left them stranded on the port. In reality, the men had reached another bay, north of the newly named San Miguel bay. It was easy to get the two bays confused; hence, it would someday be given the name "False Bay". Today, it is Mission Bay.

The journal summary is vague on the details of these events. The next morning, the men were found by another party that was sent out to search for them and guided back to the ships. Another group took a small boat and explored the large, but shallow San Miguel bay. They decided to bring two native boys with them as guides, but they couldn't communicate with the boys through sign language, so they sent them away with some shirts.

A day later, three natives came to the ships and communicated with the Spaniards by signs. They reiterated that men dressed like them had traveled further inland, riding on horses, or "caballos", but added that the men had killed many natives in those regions. They were afraid these Spaniards would do the same to them. The summary of the voyage doesn't mention what the Spanish said to the three natives, but he probably gave the natives a letter to send out to the party of Spaniards. It also tells of a heavy storm that passed over the area during Cabrillo's stay. However, the bay protected the ships so well that it passed without incident.

Cabrillo and his men stayed in San Miguel for about six days before setting sail to explore the land to the north. The trip from that point wasn't as smooth as expected though. Five months later, the San Salvador returned to San Miguel once again. Since they had last left the port, Cabrillo had died of an infected injury on some remote island and the San Salvador had become separated from the Victoria. The tired crew spent six days at the port, waiting for the other ship, which never arrived, before returning to La Paz. The Ipai and Tipai would not see a Spanish vessel again for another sixty years. In that time, parents would pass down the story of when the Guacamels visited Cosoy and the various other villages to their children and those children would grow to pass down that story to their own children. The shirts and other gifts given to the natives would rot away, the grandparents who were young adults in 1542 would die out and the stories of the Guacamels turned into legend. Other than that though, once the San Salvador left the port of San Miguel for the last time, the lives of the Ipai and Tipai would have probably gone back to normal.

What the Ipai and Tipai didn't realize was that far off in the distance and past the mountains, large and powerful cultures, represented by these visiting Guacamels, were warring with each other for world dominance, and not just dominance over land, but dominance over people and their energy. Amongst all of this warring, one of these cultures had stumbled into the native's world and was now in the process of assimilating the cultures within.

More than land and resources however, the cultures were warring over the dominance of ideas. We go through life making many decisions: Should we build arched columns or vaulted roofs? Should we speak Spanish or English? Should we follow Christianity or Islam? These decisions are deeply influenced by our cultures. The natives had similar questions: Should we build with thatch or oak? Should we speak in the dialect of the Ipai, the Tipai, or the dialect spoken by those natives living to the southeast called Kumeyaay? Did Teaipakomat really make the land out of red ants?

When cultures clash, they fight for dominance. The ancient cultures of the Ipai and Tipai have now become caught up in what has truly become a fight for world dominance. The natives and their culture were spared this time, but the differences between them and the Spanish create a problem. The natives spoke a different language than the Spanish and preferred to be mostly naked. The natives were hunters and gatherers, while the Spanish were farmers and herders. The biggest difference though: the Spanish were Christians and Christians believed that anyone who wasn't a Christian was living in sin, which meant that the Spanish saw the natives as living in sin.

In the eyes of the Spanish, it was their spiritual obligation to change the culture of the natives. In the eyes of the natives, it will someday become their spiritual obligation to preserve whatever is left of it.

Thank you for reading, visit www.aflunky.com for more information on future books and videos from Art Fusco.

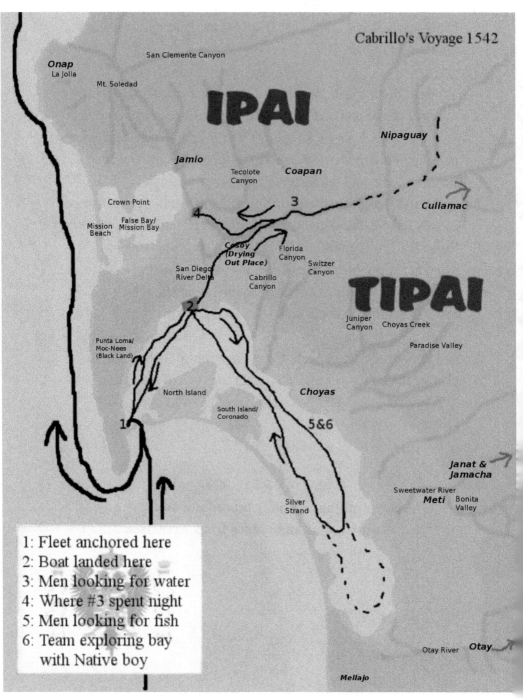

Fig 8: The route of Cabrillo and his men while visiting
San Miguel

The Following is a list of resources that helped make this story possible:

Locations:
-San Diego History Center;
Balboa Park, 1649 El Prado, San Diego, CA 92101

-San Diego Natural History Museum;
Balboa Park, 1788 El Prado, San Diego, CA 92101

-Cabrillo National Park;
1800 Cabrillo Memorial Dr, San Diego, CA 92106

-Barona Cultural Center and Museum;
1095 Barona Rd, Lakeside, CA 92040

-Battle of San Pasqual Museum;
15808 San Pasqual Valley Rd, Escondido, CA 92027

-Mission Trails Regional Park;
1 Father Junipero Serra Trail, San Diego, CA 92119

Videos:
-San Diego County Geological History;
https://www.youtube.com/watch?v=FZp0i_hIkWM

-The Rise and Fall of San Diego;
https://www.youtube.com/watch?v=-drjJoRGfAk

-First People;
http://www.pbs.org/video/2365254548/

Books:

-Susan Wise Bauer's History of the Medieval World;
http://www.susanwisebauer.com/books/history-of-the-medieval-world/

-Harry Kelsey's Juan Rodriguez Cabrillo;
http://www.amazon.com/Rodriguez-Cabrillo-Huntington-Library-Classics/dp/0873281764

-William E Smythe's History of San Diego, 1542-1908;
http://www.sandiegohistory.org/archives/books/smythe/

-Richard F. Pourade's The Explorers;
http://www.sandiegohistory.org/archives/books/explorers/

Teaching Company Courses:

-Maya to Aztec Ancient Mesoamerica revealed;
http://www.thegreatcourses.com/courses/maya-to-aztec-ancient-mesoamerica-revealed.html

-The Other 1492;
http://www.thegreatcourses.com/courses/other-1492-ferdinand-isabella-and-the-making-of-an-empire.html

PDFs galore:

-Kumeyaay History;
http://viejasbandofkumeyaay.org/wp-content/uploads/2014/10/ViejasHistoryBooklet.pdf

-Columbus' Journal;
http://www.americanjourneys.org/pdf/AJ-062.pdf

-Cannibalism?;
http://www.latinamericanstudies.org/columbus/chanca.pdf

-Relation of the Voyage of Juan Rodriguez Cabrillo;
http://www.americanjourneys.org/pdf/AJ-001.pdf

Web Pages:
-Geologic Map of San Diego;
http://www.quake.ca.gov/gmaps/RGM/sandiego/
sandiego.html

-From the San Diego Natural History Museum;
https://www.sdnhm.org/archive/research/paleontology/
sdgeol.html

-Mammoth;
http://www.foxnews.com/story/2009/02/05/mammoth-
remains-discovered-at-san-diego-construction-site.html

-Native Civilizations over time;
http://geacron.com/home-en/

-Kumeyaay History;
http://www.kumeyaay.info/history/

-Kumeyaay Timeline;
http://www.kumeyaay.com/kumeyaay-history/1-timeline.html

-Letter from Columbus to Luis de Santangel;
http://www.americanjourneys.org/aj-063/index.asp

-Letter from Columbus to Ferdinand and Isabella Concerning the Colonization and Commerce of Española;
http://www.americanjourneys.org/aj-064/index.asp

-Letter of Dr. Chanca on the Second Voyage of Columbus;
http://www.americanjourneys.org/aj-065/index.asp

-Documented Rape;
http://www.rawstory.com/2014/10/five-scary-christopher-columbus-quotes-that-let-you-celebrate-the-holiday-the-right-way/

-Florentine Codex;
https://www.historians.org/teaching-and-learning/classroom-content/teaching-and-learning-in-the-digital-age/the-conquest-of-mexico/florentine-codex

-Letters from Cortes;
https://www.historians.org/teaching-and-learning/classroom-content/teaching-and-learning-in-the-digital-age/the-conquest-of-mexico/letters-from-hernan-cortes

As well as lots of wikipedia articles:
-https://en.wikipedia.org/?title=Salton_Sink
-https://en.wikipedia.org/wiki/Washingtonia
-https://en.wikipedia.org/wiki/Fusang
-https://en.wikipedia.org/wiki/Quetzalcoatl
-https://en.wikipedia.org/wiki/Xu_Fu
-https://en.wikipedia.org/wiki/Teotihuacan
-https://en.wikipedia.org/wiki/Aztec
-https://en.wikipedia.org/wiki/Marco_Polo
-https://en.wikipedia.org/wiki/Didacus_of_Alcal%C3%A1
-https://en.wikipedia.org/wiki/Henry_IV,_Duke_of_Brunswick-L%C3%BCneburg

-https://en.wikipedia.org/wiki/Christopher_Columbus

-https://en.wikipedia.org/wiki/Voyages_of_Christopher_Columbus

-https://en.wikipedia.org/wiki/Americas#Etymology_and_naming

-https://en.wikipedia.org/wiki/Etymology_of_California

-https://en.wikipedia.org/wiki/Calafia

-https://en.wikipedia.org/wiki/Vasco_N%C3%BA%C3%B1ez_de_Balboa

-https://en.wikipedia.org/wiki/Ferdinand_Magellan

-https://en.wikipedia.org/wiki/Hern%C3%A1n_Cort%C3%A9s

-https://en.wikipedia.org/wiki/Charles_V,_Holy_Roman_Emperor

-https://en.wikipedia.org/wiki/Hernando_de_Alarc%C3%B3n

-https://en.wikipedia.org/wiki/Juan_Rodr%C3%ADguez_Cabrillo

Thanks again for reading!

CPSIA information can be obtained
at www.ICGtesting.com
Printed in the USA
BVHW042108290519
549586BV00016B/377/P

9 781366 931825